WILLIAM TYNDALE

The Teachers' Story

Terry Ellis

Brian Haddow

Jackie McWhirter

Dorothy McColgan

This book is dedicated to all those children, parents, teachers and
friends, who have supported us.

Terry Ellis, Brian Haddow, Dorothy McColgan and Jackie
McWhirter

Published 1976 by Writers and Readers Publishing Cooperative,
14 Talacre Road, London NW5 3PE

Typeset by Jetset

Printed by The Anchor Press, Tiptree, Essex

Contents

Dramatis personae

Teachers

Terry Ellis
Brian Haddow
Jackie McWhirter
Dorothy McColgan
Stevie Richards
Sheila Green
Steve Felton
Alan Head
Irene Chowles
Dolly Walker
Maureen Hercules
Brenda Hart
Margaret Ford
David Austin

Managers

Stella Burnett
Brian Tennant
Elizabeth Hoodless
Robin Mabey
Valerie Fairweather
Aelfryth Gittings
Denise Dewhurst
John Newman
John Bolland

Councillors

David Hyams
Alan Pedrick
Donald Hoodless
David Howell

M.P.s

George Cunningham
Rhodes Boyson

Inner London Education Authority

Members
Ashley Bramall
Harvey Hinds
Anne Page
Jenny Baker

Officials
Eric Briault
Michael Birchenough
Vivian Pape
Donald Rice
Laurie Buxton
Hedley Wales
Norman Kalber
John Welch

National Union of Teachers

Horace Perrin
Fred Jarvis
Fred Smith
Ron Lendon

Inquiry

Dora Loftus
Robin Auld
George Carter

Introduction

On Thursday October 16th 1975, seven London primary school teachers returned after a three week strike to what had been labelled 'The School of Shame'. A damning report from a team of inspectors who had never seen any of these teachers at work had been leaked to the press by the school's managers. Whipped up by national headlines, angry parents picketed the school threatening to lynch the seven. Only fifty children remained from what had been over two hundred two years previously. This day saw the climax of eighteen months' harassment of William Tyndale Junior school. The public inquiry followed a week later, and for four months, at enormous expense, attempted to rationalise this breakdown in the English schooling system.

There have been many versions of the events at Tyndale. This is the first opportunity for some of those who actually taught there to give their side of the story and their own analysis of the conflict. This book is a cooperative venture written as a chronological account woven around several chapters commenting upon the forces which seek to control teachers and what they teach. Many events were unknown to the teachers at the time of happening and only emerged in the inquiry. They therefore form a 'hidden' chronology. It is possible to read this book in two ways — either sequentially or by taking the narrative of events as a whole and leaving the chapters of analysis until last.

At the time of writing, the inquiry report has not been published. The teachers remain on voluntary leave until their future has been decided.

Chapter 1
Before January 1974

William Tyndale School stands back from Upper Street, Islington, London, wedged ominously between the Town Hall and Divisional Office, the centre of educational administration for the district which has been at the heart of other educational controversies, including the famous Risinghill. The building is unimpressive; built in 1916, it is of a large three-decker Victorian type. The interior is cheerless. In a report made during the inspection in September 1975, the art inspector aptly describes the route to the Junior School, which mainly occupies the top floor of the building: 'the Junior School can be approached by two stairways, both are built of dark brown brickwork and have a depressing feeling'. The corridors are equally gloomy, the bottom half of the walls being built of the same dark brickwork; and the classrooms are small.

The area surrounding the school is one of contrasts. On one side of Upper Street lies the Barnsbury district, with its abundance of costly Georgian houses, on the other, Tyndale Mansions and Canonbury Court, ageing blocks of Council flats. The former are expensively renovated by the fashionable middle classes moving into the area, the latter left undisturbed, with a concentration of poorer families. The influx of professional people with above average incomes has produced a fall in population. The aspiring working class have moved out, or try to move out, to better accommodation in the suburbs, and the previously multi-occupied houses have become owner occupied, housing one family instead of several. This has produced a fall in the numbers at local schools of about 8% per year over the whole borough, and will cause the closure of some schools.

Conditions in the Council flats have not changed: dingy stairs littered with rubbish; families with insufficient space and inadequate facilities.

With the removal of one section of the population, the former working class community has changed. The area has been left to richer and poorer. Any community spirit which might have existed has disappeared and been replaced by a rivalry, not only between but also within differing social groupings, as the desire to 'better oneself' is nourished. Working-class groups seem unaware they have similar interests. The English residents are led to believe their problems are increased by the immigrant population who take up valuable jobs and accommodation, rather than by the middle class. This breeds resentment and encourages in-fighting, instead of a combined attack on conditions. People try to get on at the expense of their immediate neighbours, and there is antagonism from those who do not make it.

In such an area of social mix, educational problems arise. The pressures put on local schools highlight the contradictions of a community school system, which should encourage the integration of differing groups by catering for *all* children in the area. The middle class, with their better conditions, are able to take more interest in their children's education. They have more time and confidence to visit the school and attend functions than the often tired and overworked working class parent. They are also more articulate and vociferous. The inarticulate parent is intimidated by them, particularly at parents' meetings. Parent-teacher associations can become middle class dominated, and the working class parent discouraged from attending meetings. The middle class therefore have greater influence on how the school is run.

Community schools in areas of social mix often yield to these pressures, so that schools are run for the middle classes at the expense of the socially deprived child. Children with the difficulties associated with living in poor conditions in an inner urban area are,

2

at best, merely coped with, and sometimes removed to special schools. Other working class children are encouraged to compete, both academically and socially. They are presented with middle class values and codes of conduct. This can only lead to the bourgeoisification of the working class. The children themselves do not mix. Instead of playing and working with their peer group, Tyndale children tended to play with their social group.

The middle class favours a more progressive approach to education, the working class emphasises discipline and the '3 R's'. At secondary level this leads to a 'split' system, with the middle-class favouring certain schools, the working class others. Whilst most working-class parents in Islington want their children to attend a more formal, single sex school, the middle class parent searches for a more 'liberal' institution.

At primary level the situation is different. The working-class parent favours the nearest school available, the middle-class parent shops around before choosing. Different schools are 'in vogue' at different times: in the late 1960s Tyndale had attracted a larger percentage of middle class children than its catchment area justified.

Alan Head took over at the Junior School in 1968. He had previously been deputy head of a local school; this was his first headship. The Infant School had also had a new head, Brenda Hart, the previous year. In her statement to the inquiry she commented that when she arrived: 'They were very separate schools. This does not mean that there was discord between the two heads, but there was apparently a lack of liaison on educational matters. I noticed this particularly in the matter of the lack of continuity in reading schemes'. There was also no post of responsibility for liaison between the schools.

Both schools had been run on fairly traditional lines, both heads wanted to introduce new 'progressive' policies. There were some transitional difficulties. Hart was to describe how children would sometimes wander into the playground and disrupt other children's work, so that she enforced stricter boundaries. Some parents also complained about the new methods. Even so, by 1973, Hart had a stable staff who shared her ideas, and a school which was popular with the middle classes.

Although the Junior School's image of a successful modern school still persists, the transition there did not proceed so smoothly. Head wanted to introduce more informal teaching, particularly team teaching. He tried to gather round him a staff who shared his ideas, preferring to work with young, progressive teachers. He succeeded in this at first. The deputy head was Irene Chowles, who had worked at the school before his arrival. She was a 'formal' teacher, and this led to some conflict. And though the school was thought to be run on progressive lines, there were no organisational policies. Teachers worked in separate classrooms in any way they wished. As is normal in most comparable schools no clear indications of what they taught, or how it should be taught, were given. There was no generally agreed and stated curriculum.

In November 1973 District Inspector Laurie Buxton, then responsible for Tyndale, made a report on the school to the committee which was to appoint the new head. This stated that Head had 'established a style of approach that is extremely forward looking, organised and cohesive'. It is easy to understand the anger of some Tyndale staff in 1975 at being criticised for a lack of organisation and curriculum.

Staff meetings in Head's time were the exception rather than the rule. Their function was to discuss dates of routine events such as the Summer Fair or Christmas parties, rather than the running of the school or any underlying philosophy. Consultation with staff, even on minor issues, was minimal. Instructions to staff were often accompanied by the words 'you are professionals'. This put the onus for the school s problems on the individual teachers, and any failures down to individual inadequacies and inabilities. No collective responsibility was encouraged. Yet, according to Buxton's report, Head 'exercised a firm and positive, democratic leadership'.

Team teaching was introduced for a while, but only to a limited degree. It could more accurately be described as co-operative teaching, as it usually involved private arrangements between staff. One co-operative project that was started, with the assistance of Head, petered out in a few weeks. The results of the methods employed encouraged staff to compete with each other. Great emphasis was given to work visually pleasing to the casual observer; the classroom displays were the responsibility of the individual teachers. This, together with the fact that blame was apportioned to teachers who could not contain their problems within their classrooms, kindled the competitive spirit. Some teachers tried to hoard equipment in an attempt to 'better their results'. Teachers tended to court parental support for their own methods, rather than

4

for the whole school. In addition, the school had little basic equipment: staff were constantly borrowing to supplement their alloted six rulers and scissors per class of thirty. Was this the same school Buxton described as 'a thriving establishment to take over, the staff will respond well'?

Why did the outside world have such a rosy picture? Head was a talented teacher, adept at public relations. He played the guitar at assemblies, which impressed parents. Before inspectors visited he expected staff to put more work on display. He sometimes taught groups of children for this purpose. Entertainments were staged twice a year for parents. All the children from each class were involved (even though staff were only allowed £1 per class to provide them with costumes). There were numerous out of school activities, including concerts and involvement in T.V. programmes, all things impressive to an outsider. The school was often visited by students. Courses were held there, enabling Head to explain his ideas to other teachers, even if these ideas were not being extended into the classroom. Tyndale, in reality no more than a typical London school, appeared as one of exceptional achievement.

No one began to look any closer until 1972. During 1971-72 six full-time and one part-time teachers left, out of a staff of ten. It was the ones attracted by the school image, the 'progressive' teachers, who left, leaving Head with the most 'formal' staff. The 'progressives' were to be replaced by more 'formal' teachers. 1972-73 started without a full complement of staff; two full-time teachers were missing. One was replaced immediately by a long-term supply teacher, the other by a series of supply teachers, until a more permanent solution was found in 1973.

Peter Wetz, a newly qualified primary teacher, was put in charge of a first-year team. He was assisted by Sheila Green, who had come as a supply teacher the previous year, and by Maureen Hercules, a part-time teacher with children in the Infants'. One of the two classes involved had had an unsettled time as the top Infant class, and their parents were concerned about the team teaching. Some felt a 'difficult' class should have the security of a classroom teacher, others that their children would be disturbed by the inclusion of the more disruptive class in the team. The team turned out to be a form of streaming, with Green taking the 'brighter' children, and Wetz the others. The classes initially without permanent teachers were also having problems, particularly with children disturbed by constant changes of temporary staff.

In 1973 Head was appointed headmaster of a new school in Oxfordshire. By this time some parents, no longer convinced by pretty work, had become even more dissatisfied. In his evidence to the inquiry Stuart Behrman, a parent, said he removed his child in 1972 because others were removing theirs, and his daughter was becoming isolated from the 'brighter' children. Whilst still praising the efforts of Head, he said he did not like the 'decline'. Others had similar feelings, and the roll dropped by 32 that year.

Head left Tyndale in July 1973. Due to a shortage of suitable candidates no new head was immediately appointed. Buxton told Chowles he would bring in an acting head from outside, but she preferred to take the job, as was her right. There was one additional problem for Head's successor, which was to take on significance later. An arrangement was made between Jean Donnison, then Chairman of Managers, Buxton, who was soon to leave his post, and Head, to allow Wetz to work half time at the local teachers' centre as deputy warden, and half time at Tyndale taking a first-year class. Hercules was to take this class for the other half of the week. An arrangement like this, particularly with a first-year class, which needs stability during the transition from Infants to Juniors, is never satisfactory. Those involved in setting it up never had the responsibility for carrying it through.

In September 1973 Chowles became acting head. There were three new members of staff. Stevie Richards was to start her probationary year, taking a first-year class. Brian Haddow had four years' teaching experience in London, and had been told by Buxton that the school was run on team-teaching lines that would suit Haddow's style. Jackie McWhirter had worked at the school previously, but had been abroad for a year. All three favoured 'progressive' methods. Of the staff who remained at the school Green was 'progressive', Ruby Ranasinghe, Sue Fox, Wetz, Hercules and Dolly Walker 'formal' teachers. Walker, a part-time remedial reading teacher, had worked at the school for five years. She had previously attacked a former member of the staff for his progressive methods, and had even told parents that their children had regressed since being in his class. She was later in the term to attack Hart's methods in the Infant School, and to prepare a document criticising

6

the Infants.

Chowles had inherited many problems; her period of acting headship was to produce more. She immediately tried to introduce more rigid structures. The staff resented the extra pressures put on them as more rules were introduced. As there was still no definite school policy, the more traditional teachers were encouraged by the new disciplinary methods to oppose the 'progressive' elements. The atmosphere became unpleasant: arguments erupted, there was constant bickering. Chowles was often at the centre of arguments.

There were additional problems with the Wetz/Hercules class. Hercules was having difficulties coping. On November 20th 1973 she left for Australia, informing nobody at the school of her departure, her whereabouts, or her date of return. She left her children at the school, her son being in her own class. An unsatisfactory situation became extremely difficult. As replacements are not permitted for staff working part-time the class was left with no teacher for half the week, a gap which had to be covered by other members of staff. Parents again thought about removing their children because of the staffing situation.

In November the staff decided to withdraw from dinner duties — a move within their contract, and within NUT policy. The decision was unanimous, and extra dinner supervisors were employed. Chowles asked Haddow, as acting deputy head, to draft a letter to Divisional Office stating the staff's decision. This letter was later to be used against some of the teachers.

Equipment was still short, even though Chowles was ordering new stock. She felt the school was always chasing basic necessities, and was therefore unable to build up a store of equipment. There were some staff absences through illness, and despite the new rules behaviour problems continued. Two children were suspended by Chowles for violent behaviour during this term.

The managers were taking a greater interest in the school. During Head's time managers rarely visited. Caryl Harter, parent manager from 1971 to 1973, told the inquiry that when she had attended managers' meetings they had discussed toilets, school dinners, but little more: they had taken no interest in the running of the school. In autumn 1973 the managing body was re-constituted. The new chairwoman, Stella Burnett, Aelfryth Gittings, with two children in the school, and the newly elected parent manager, Denise Dewhurst, visited the school more frequently. (It was during one of Dewhurst's visits, so she told the inquiry, that Chowles told her Haddow was a 'Trot'.)

By the end of term Chowles was finding it difficult to cope. The staff were divided, and in the main unsympathetic to her running of the school. It no longer even gave the appearance of operating smoothly. Chowles applied for the headship when it was advertised again, but the managers did not include her among the three candidates sent to County Hall for final interview. Terry Ellis was appointed in November 1973, and took over in January 1974. He was not informed in advance of the fall in the roll, nor of the divisions between staff. An angry parents' meeting, held in November 1973, had revealed hostility towards the Juniors, and unfair comparisons had been drawn between it and the Infants'. Parents and some managers were now scrutinising the school, looking for some sort of miracle.

Chapter 2
The Role of the Head

The ILEA always thoroughly vets potential head teachers. The scheme operated in the early 1970s was in two stages. Candidates for headships appeared for assessment before two boards, consisting of inspectors and officers of the authority. Only after clearing these obstacles could the candidate be admitted to the 'promotion list'. Unless admitted, they were not eligible even to apply for headships. The two boards which, in 1970 and 1971, recommended Ellis for the promotion list contained three inspectors who participated in the Tyndale affair. Buxton, Pape and Welch all agreed Ellis had good headship potential.

Early in 1972 Ellis began the second stage. This consisted of interviews by the managing bodies of schools for whose headships he applied, leading to a short list, considered by the Appointment of Head Teachers section of the staff and General Purposes Sub-Committee of the ILEA. Thus, when Ellis became head, his appointment had been endorsed by four lay and professional committees. The complexity of the ILEA screening process is designed in part to ensure unwanted candidates do not get through. What Ellis did not know at the time was that one of those at the final interview did not want him appointed. Jenny Baker, an

Islington resident and influential member of the minority
Conservative group on the ILEA Education Committee, would not
normally have been present, but on this occasion attended and
recorded her objection to Ellis. Ellis did not know that the
managers, though short-listing three candidates for further
interview, had expressed no preference. The headship had been first
advertised in June 1973; although Ellis had applied and been
interviewed, the appointment process was halted because of
managerial reluctance. He was told this was due to a shortage of
suitable candidates.

Ellis visited the school in summer 1973, and was surprised it had
such a high reputation in the locality. It seemed little different from
many other London schools he had seen. The building was drab and
bare, staff turnover had been high, and the problems inherent in
inner-city areas were everywhere to be seen. There were also hints of
a poor relationship between Head and deputy head Chowles. The
problems did not inhibit Ellis from making a second application: no
applicant for a London headship expects an easy school. The readvertisement brought a 'field' of nineteen candidates.

Ellis, of working class origin, was educated at Parmiter's
Foundation and King's College, London. After graduation he spent
two years teaching abroad, before returning to work for the ILEA
in East London. Moving to Islington as deputy head of Charles Lamb
Junior School, he helped set up team teaching there. Both as a
teacher and deputy head he was highly successful: at the inquiry
tribute to his work was paid by his former head at Charles Lamb,
Philip Clark.

Charles Lamb School is near Tyndale, and many of its pupils
have the same problems. Whilst at Charles Lamb Ellis wrote a
substantial study on team teaching, as part of his work for the post-
graduate Diploma in Primary Education he obtained in 1971. Some
of the team teaching work was videotaped by the ILEA, for use in
teacher training courses. Ellis, therefore, has some claim to expertise
in team teaching — far more than many inspectors who were to
assess Tyndale.

From September 1971 to July 1972 Ellis was acting head of
Charles Lamb whilst it was being re-organised; he became deputy
head when the school moved into its open-plan building in
September 1972. Ellis and his colleagues worked hard during its
transition from the traditional closed classrooms to a more open

10

and flexible system, based on team and co-operative teaching techniques.

Ellis is a teacher in the 'progressive' mould, although he had begun to see limitations in the forms of primary education practised in the 1960s. He had lost faith in the idea that schools could be used for social engineering, and was moving to the view that the system placed a strain on the relationship between adult and child which often nullified most of what the teacher was trying to achieve. In particular, he felt the need to discriminate in favour of the disadvantaged child, who lacks the family and social support most middle class children enjoy.

At the inquiry middle-class witnesses accused Ellis and the teachers of neglecting the 'gifted' child (they meant the middle-class child), of concentrating on the poor and immigrant pupils. An accusation of racial discrimination was levelled against the school, because it devoted extra attention to the West Indian, Greek and Turkish children, who had the greatest problems. When alleged cases of indiscipline by children were raised at the inquiry, they usually involved black children.

Whilst some middle-class parents objected to what they claimed was an excessive concentration on the socially deprived child, some working-class parents saw the same actions as treating the children in the way middle-class children are treated. One working-class Labour Party member said; 'I feel Ellis is a marvellous teacher for middle-class children'. He appeared to mean that it was alright to reason with such children, and to encourage them to achieve autonomy, but the workers' child needs to be directed and led.

Ellis had a reputation for being frank and outspoken, though this has been exaggerated (perhaps he was just frank and outspoken to the wrong people). He was prepared to discuss his ideas, and since some were not conventional there was always the danger he might be misunderstood. Ellis rejected the autocratic concept of the head's role, and introduced at Tyndale the idea of policy decisions being discussed by the whole staff acting as a committee, with regular and lengthy meetings.

Staff participation in decision making is anathema to many powerful and influential people in education. In 1973 the Executive of the National Union of Teachers rejected, almost out of hand, a report of a union working party, which recommended a marginal degree of staff involvement in decision making. Since many administrators and head teachers cannot conceive of relinquishing any powers, Ellis's action could only be explained by these people as a submission to pressure from staff.

Vivian Pape, who was in charge of the inspection which preceded the inquiry, made it clear that he found it remarkable a head might wish to share his power. A number of hostile witnesses at the inquiry clearly saw any 'democratic' relationship between head and staff as not only unacceptable, but an overtly political act. Right-wing newspapers went even further, accusing the school of operating as a revolutionary commune. Almost without exception, those who attacked Ellis for betraying the 'leadership principle' on which the English school system is based would declare themselves to be convinced democrats. Yet the same people bitterly oppose any change in which the opinions of class teachers carry no less but no more weight than that of a head.

It is argued that English schools are protected from the centralised direction and uniform curricula typical of Continental countries because of the autonomy granted to head teachers. Much was made of this by Harvey Hinds, ILEA Schools Sub-Committee Chairman, who argued that our system was superior because direction and control was placed in the hands of the head and the managers or governors. But Ellis and the school came to grief because this theory does not accord with the practice. Power is granted to heads only so long as they exercise it in accordance with the wishes of the political masters.

When the inquiry was set up it was done as an exercise in accountability—yet the ILEA inspectorate were opposed to their reports on the school becoming public in the inquiry. They argued such publicity would destroy the delicate professional relationship between inspectors and teachers. Why the relationship, if genuine, should be delicate rather than robust, was never explained. For many teachers, including Ellis and his staff, the inspectorate are merely the medium through which control is exerted, by the authority, over the school.

The machinery of control is spelled out in the Education Act of 1944, and in the Articles of Management of the school. According to the Act, the authority shall determine the educational character of the school; subject to this the managers shall have the general direction of the conduct and curriculum. The managers are required to act in consultation with the head, who 'shall control the conduct

12

and curriculum, the internal organisation, management and discipline of the school, the choice of equipment, books and other resources, the methods of teaching and the general arrangement of teaching groups, and shall exercise supervision over the teaching and non-teaching staff'

This quotation is from the Rules of Management of an Inner London County Primary School, and is a typical statement of the powers conferred on a head. Normally the head is free to make whatever changes he wishes in the curriculum and conduct of the school, subject only to consultation with the managers. Since the majority of school managers have little knowledge of education, control remains in the hands of the head, *so long as he does not come into conflict with authority*. When a conflict arises, the rules, by their lack of definition, do not give a clear indication of where responsibility and power lie.

The normal state of affairs is advantageous not only to heads, but to the education authorities themselves. As a matter of 'professional courtesy' inspectors pass on to heads their advice on educational matters, and on the way the school should be conducted. They never instruct directly, but merely offer 'help'. H.R. Chetwynd, former head of Woodberry Down Comprehensive, London, now an ILEA Staff Inspector, wrote in *Comprehensive School:* 'While I have received much help for which I have asked from the Council, its officers and inspectors, I have never received what I consider to be a directive, much less a blueprint!'

The head who accepts this 'help' obviously conducts a school in a manner that meets with approval at County Hall; but this 'help' extends beyond the technical issues of education. Senior ILEA officers and inspectors have made their views known on what they believe to be ideological matters. Education Officer Eric Briault has said publicly he believes it wrong to question middle-class values relating to the conduct and behaviour of children. Assistant Education Officer Don Venvell has spoken disapprovingly about the fact that arguments on trade union issues are now common in many staffrooms.

Such views are not uncommon in any hierarchical organisation, but the structure of the school administrative system ensures that the holders of these views can have them propagated at classroom level. Any head advised that County Hall looks with disfavour on particular activities, will do his best to minimise those activities, if he wishes to retain the confidence and support of the administration. If, in the eyes of the authority, a head challenges the value judgements of the administrators, confidence and support is withdrawn.

The Tyndale case demonstrates that the power of the head is a fiction, that it rests on the prop of the authority. Once the prop is removed the head and the school face almost certain disaster. Inspectors do not issue directives, at least not in a form that can be identified as a directive, so the removal of support does not become immediately obvious to those working in a school.

Before Ellis arrived at the school the staff's activities had attracted the attention of Divisional Office. During autumn 1973 the staff had indicated that they no longer wished to continue dinner duties. During the same term a number of the staff had signed a letter to the Authority indicating their support for Dorothy McColgan in her dispute with the Authority (see page 19). Both these actions were legitimate. When Ellis arrived at the start of 1974 the school was operating an official NUT sanction, declining to cover for staff absent for more than three days. The sanction, designed to support the current London Allowance campaign by the Union, was operating in North London secondary schools, but Tyndale was one of the few primary schools to support the campaign in this way. Other primary heads ignored Union policy. Nothing was ever said to Ellis about these matters by any inspector, but they were raised by both the ILEA and the managers during the inquiry. It will never be known what influence these actions had on the divisional officers since the divisional officer and his deputy refused to give evidence to the inquiry.

During Ellis's first term no inspector visited the school. Buxton, who was responsible for the school, knew that he would be handing over his responsibility in March. Ellis and his deputy, Chowles, had had disagreements with Buxton well before 1974. The first visit came in April 1974, when Inspector Donald Rice, now District Inspector, in his first month with the ILEA, came to see Ellis. Later in the month McColgan was appointed by a full managers' meeting. This appointment, which was a promotion for McColgan, was made with Ellis's agreement. It caused the school to be viewed with further suspicion, as McColgan had been out of favour with the authority for some years.

During May 1974 events moved into a pattern which has become almost classic in those cases where a head has made a definite moves towards a more democratic set-up, and a greater degree of attention to the socially deprived child. The pattern begins with teachers, often senior members of staff, going behind the head's back to the inspectors or officers of the authority. Contacts are made, in secret, with managers, councillors and politicians. These actions are usually a breach of authority rules, and contrary to the professional conduct code of the NUT.

The information fed to the teacher's contacts is invariably about alleged misconduct, indiscipline and vandalism. Much is made of dress styles of the younger teachers, and remarks, torn from their context of staffroom discussion, are retailed as evidence of subversive intentions condoned by the head.

Teachers who go behind the head's back are never the subject of sanctions or reproof from those to whom they tell tales. Once the first step has been taken the pace quickens. Gossip spreads amongst parents, and is given authenticity because it comes from persons officially connected with the school. Information is passed to the press, and when possible, as it was at Tyndale, stories are passed up the political ladder to the highest level.

The following chapters will show how this pattern operated in summer 1974. Whatever reasons the authority had for this attitude towards Ellis, the secret dealings of the managers, Walker, Infant staff and the ILEA were actions that increased the school's problems; constructive help must of necessity be in the open. We must therefore look for reasons for this attitude which are equally not out in the open; ample evidence of those will be found as the story unfolds.

They mirror in a great deal of detail two recent cases of heads removed from their posts — Michael Duane of Risinghill School in Islington and Gerry German of Mold Comprehensive in Flintshire. All three heads had a concern for the socially deprived child which could not be challenged. They shared a desire to see their schools operating as communities, based on practices which were as democratic as possible.

Duane knew when he started at Risinghill that there had been a political battle, in which he was not involved, over the siting of the school. There were, therefore, those who had a vested interest in seeing the school fail. It might have succeeded, because Duane had the support of a sympathetic chairman of governors. However, she was replaced by an ex School Inspector. Duane found, as did Ellis, that the task of getting the school together was difficult when managers or governors and the administration opposed the head.

What of the support heads receive from other head teachers? Ellis was never included in the 'inner circle' of local heads. There is a close connection between heads who are NUT members; although Ellis was in the union, he was never admitted to the circle, because the idea of staff participation in decision-making was resisted there. Ellis was also not invited to, or informed of, some of the meetings and activities of the local joint consultative committee of heads. Comparing Ellis's position with that of other heads who have attracted publicity is illuminating. When the Chris Searle case arose in East London, local heads supported Geoffrey Barrell, head of Searle's school, and pledged they would ensure Searle would not be employed in the division. Searle's offence was not to slander his head, but to publish his children's poetry without Barrell's consent.

One lesson of Tyndale is that the power of the head teacher is illusory. Any head who fails to obey orders is courting disaster. Of course, the word 'order' is never used. The chairman of managers chats over a glass of sherry, and the inspector over lunch on the head's desk, and no 'directive' is ever issued. It does not need to be. Most head teachers recognise they are the servants of those who employ them, and would never dream of countering their master's implied wishes. The needs and wishes of children and parents come a poor second. Any head who fails to defer is discarded.

Chapter 3
January–July 1974

New head teachers normally proceed with caution. Ellis was no exception. But it was obvious some kind of school policy needed hammering out. However much staff might look at the head to sense the direction in which he was moving, they themselves would want a say in the decisions taken. Ellis therefore set up, in the form of a weekly staff-meeting, a forum where developments could be discussed and group decisions taken, by vote if necessary.

Such a forum imposes responsibility. It demands a willingness to accept majority decisions, to grant respect to others' views, and a desire to talk out matters in dispute. The Tyndale decision-making process led to allegations from both inspectors and Chowles that Ellis was not acting as the 'head', that is, not following the normal leader-principle on which most schools are run. Chowles' objections are weakened by the fact that she had criticized Head for being too authoritarian with staff.

But the immediate problem was the absence of Hercules. There was no indication of when she intended to return. In order to get a replacement, Ellis, with the support of Buxton, terminated her contract. Her place was taken by a succession of supply teachers; the 'split' class remained like a running sore in the side of the school.

It soon became obvious the forum was providing Walker with an arena for the propagation of her own ideas, to the exclusion of most other matters. Discussions had been undertaken about the future direction of the school, and Walker opposed vehemently any 'progressive' views, particularly from Ellis, Haddow or McWhirter. She became increasingly animated as she failed to convince them, or, eventually, to carry the majority of staff. She believed Ellis and Haddow to be politically motivated in the ideas they put forward. Though she mostly concealed this at the time, occasional outbursts revealed her thinking. Haddow was told to 'go and throw bombs', and the mildly expressed view that children should be allowed to eat sweets was countered by Walker's assertion that this practice would lead to drug addiction.

By April 1974, a rift was developing between Walker and other members of staff. She had decided those opposing her were out to bring down society, a matter she was to elaborate on to others outside the school. This outside communication is the key to some of the early tribulations of Tyndale. There are violent disputes in many staffrooms: they mostly stay there. Walker took her one-sided version of the debate into a much wider arena.

One universally agreed matter was that links with parents needed strengthening. Much has been made of the alleged lack of parental involvement at Tyndale. Yet from the beginning Ellis contacted parents by every means available. The inquiry documents are full of his letters. A newsletter, compiled by parent-manager Dewhurst, who was aided by Haddow, gave information about the school, and requested help in making it more attractive physically. The classroom behaviour of one child was vastly improved by inviting his mother to come and work with him. Several mothers came regularly to help teachers in class.

Haddow, when projecting a change of direction with his class, sent a letter to all his parents, seeking their opinions and inviting them to see his work. He followed this with a questionnaire asking for an assessment of this work. Teachers rarely undertake this sort of step. The response was minimal—which makes it all the more strange that the conduct of Haddow's class came in for more criticism than any other. A parents' meeting was held in the first term to explain aspects of future policy; mainly the organisation for teaching literacy. Teachers even went to parents' homes in the evenings to persuade as many as possible to attend.

18

There was much talk in the inquiry about parental anxiety at this time. In fact, Ellis had inherited parental anxiety. He had assumed that, because the school had a progressive image, making modern methods understandable to parents had already largely been done. This was not so. But, whatever the circumstances of the school, heads are allowed a chance to develop their own policies. Ellis was not afforded this opportunity. Norma Heigham, an Infant parent, told the inquiry she was approached, only weeks after Ellis had arrived, by a local 'political' figure (whom she would not name), who made strong criticisms of his conduct of the school.

Haddow was elected teacher-manager in January, joining Ellis, who was already a member of the managing body by virtue of his office. Relationships with the few managers that came to the school were cordial. Ellis was happy to let them visit at will, and did not subject them to the usual 'guided tour'. Chairwoman Burnett and managers Gittings and Dewhurst, both with children in the school, were frequent, and at first welcome, visitors. Ellis discussed his educational ideas and plans, emphasizing that staff needed time to implement them. The managing body, at its January meeting, passed a resolution of support for an increased London allowance. In May, Dewhurst sought parental support for this by canvassing a petition among parents. Some managers later claimed that strife was caused by Ellis's failure to communicate with them. It might be more just to claim the opposite. He refused to mystify them, or enter into the image-making process most heads use, and was frank about the difficulties of inner-city education.

The staffing of the 'split' class was clearly a source of parental anxiety. A solution suggested itself when Wetz was appointed to a full-time post at the local teachers' centre at Easter. McWhirter agreed to take this class, and assume responsibility for liaison with the Infants', with whom joint staff meetings had been agreed. A new teacher, with special responsibility for mathematics, needed to be appointed.

One applicant for the post was Dorothy McColgan, a well-known figure in North London. A former President of the NLTA, she was known as an active campaigner for greater teacher participation in decision-making. She was a member of Rank and File, an activist group of NUT members, which was not favoured by either the NUT leadership or ILEA. She had come into conflict with ILEA in 1969, and the dispute, never fully resolved, had flared up again in 1973 when Buxton, one of the original participants, had tried to transfer her from her school. She had refused, amid considerable publicity, and had not held a post since September 1973. She had visited Tyndale, among other schools, that autumn, to seek support in her fight.

The managers appointed her. They later claimed their information about her past had been insufficient; but when she volunteered it at the time, they declined her offer.

In February Haddow approached Ellis about new directions for his class, involving a wider range of options and a more fluid use of space. Another innovation was 'language groups', an attempt to induce greater co-operation among teachers, and to make an assault on the literacy problem. Walker had previously had sole charge of remedial reading, but low reading standards were so widespread, especially among children recently transferred from the Infants', that an attack on a broad front was necessary. The staff agreed on this, though Walker nursed a resentment that her remedial empire had been dismantled. The change of policy was carefully prepared. A senior remedial teacher was invited to the school; the matter was discussed with parents; a more modern reading test was introduced, to be used later to monitor progress.

Buxton had been promoted in January, and was replaced in March by Rice, formerly chief inspector for the borough of Kingston, and before that, an inspector and head in Essex. He had no recent teaching experience, nor knew the ways of the strife-ridden Islington division—although he was surrounded by colleagues who knew the ropes better than most.

On April 1st, Rice made his first visit to the school. Ellis outlined his plans, which Rice pronounced as thoroughly sound. Ellis also gave a full explanation of the divisions among staff.

The triumvirate of power that controls the destiny of a school usually consists of the head, the inspector, and the chairman of managers. When a school encounters difficulties, concerted action on the part of these is usually enough to ensure a resolution of problems. But at Tyndale all three were comparatively new to their jobs, and inexperienced in their particular functions. The situation was ripe for anyone wishing to manipulate it.

When term ended, there were anxieties about staff divisions, and the first hints of managerial pressure (from Gittings and Dewhurst), but still no reason to believe that optimism was

20

misplaced. As the staff went on holiday they had no idea of the storm about to break.

Things began quietly. There was now more obvious movement in the school. Haddow's class was making use of the previously barren hall. The new reading organisation, involving children moving to other groups for an hour each day, had its teething troubles; many children from formal classrooms were unused to fluidity. The school was into a transitional stage, which any system has to go through in order to achieve a relaxed atmosphere and true development, as distinct from a 'holding operation' designed to present an image of spurious control. The school needed quiet support from its managers and a chance to prove itself. This was the opposite to what it would get.

Towards the end of May, the first small detonations in the coming chain reaction made themselves heard. On May 16th Burnett visited the school, and expressed her satisfaction. On June 3rd a second visit produced statements of extreme concern, of having received expressions of worry and criticism from managers and parents. Why this change of attitude?

A joint Infant-Junior staff meeting had been held in April. It had been cordial, a social occasion. Differences of approach had been more apparent between members of the Junior staff than the two staffs as a whole. Yet on May 20th, when Rice visited the Infants', he was greeted with a series of complaints about the Juniors.

On May 22nd Walker produced for the first time in public one of her documents — a paper extremely critical of school policy. Personal attacks were made on Ellis and McWhirter, 'chaos and anarchy' were said to be in possession, and 'half-baked psychological ideas' were castigated. She proposed to call her own parents' meeting. Haddow, later to rate so high in Walker's demonology, was only mentioned because he talked of 'children's rights', a phrase that assumed greater significance later. Walker proved to be a great producer of documents in varying drafts, and this one had been prepared over a period of time.

McWhirter had taken over some of Walker's remedial readers, and worked next door to her. Her manner of working did not fit in with the Walker philosophy—McWhirter believed in building the child's confidence before an assault on the academic problem was made. Haddow worked in a different part of the building, and

Walker knew nothing of his methods, although she had already objected violently to his expressed philosophy. She visited his classroom in his absence and observed what was displayed on the walls. At this point, Haddow's famous 'tigers' come growling on to the scene. This event provides a prime illustration of how something completely harmless can be twisted by distortion and gossip to a point where it seems a danger to the whole fabric of a school.

Haddow had suggested, as a subject for painting, among many others, a quotation from William Blake: 'The Tigers of wrath are wiser than the horses of instruction' (Walker claimed 'destruction' had replaced 'wrath'). In the game of Chinese whispers that ensued, the words reached parents and managers as 'the tigers of destruction are more beautiful than the horses of industry', or even 'the horses of revolution are more powerful than the forces of education'. The phrase reached its apotheosis a year later in the *Daily Mail*, as 'the smile on the face of the tiger is revolution', an alleged utterance of Chairman Mao.

Walker carried her version off to Rice some time in May, without approaching Haddow, before or after. Rice apparently took little notice, and never came to either Ellis or Haddow for an explanation. Nobody ever did, and the rumours circulated. This was the germination of the 'political indoctrination' myth.

The political question has been carefully skirted by most commentaries on Tyndale. There has been no shortage of 'red-baiting' from the usual quarters, nor of implications that children were being corrupted by revolutionaries. But many 'serious', liberal-minded commentators have avoided the politics altogether, probably because of a fear of being enticed into dangerous waters where it might be necessary to let the general public know that all education has a political basis.

The debate has been carefully led into 'what went on in the classroom', on the grounds that this is what influences people's views of a school. Yet most people (inspectors, managers, parents and, above all, journalists) have no idea what does go on in classrooms. Schools exist on the projection of images, often no true reflection of reality. This deception is known as public relations.

Teachers have a function in society quite separate from their technical one. The stances they appear to adopt in areas separated, in the eyes of the public, from their teaching and child-minding functions, can assume a vast importance. Some Tyndale staff had taken up, and were to take up again, positions on certain issues, that created a 'political image'. It is a major part of their case that this image did as much, if not more, than their educational practice, in bringing about the attacks on them.

On May 23rd the majority of Tyndale teachers, including Ellis, went on 'unofficial' strike over their London allowance. This was only one of a series of stances which were to convince many that Tyndale was dominated by a dangerous political faction, that the head was a weakling being manipulated for political ends. The teachers had already opted out of dinner duty, an action not understood by ancillary helpers or parents, who saw lunch-time supervision as part of a teacher's natural job.

Haddow, McWhirter, Richards and Green had all supported McColgan in the past, and now she was on the staff. The whole staff had followed to the letter the NUT policy on not 'covering' for absent colleagues. Classes had been sent home when replacement teachers were not available, which had already prompted one parent to call Ellis 'a bloody communist'.

Teachers are expected to be martinets with children, but easily cowed by adults. Many Tyndale teachers acted and talked like trade unionists, an apparently unexceptionable attitude in factory workers or miners, but rather shocking in a profession renowned for its docility. Radical educational ideas were being discussed in the staffroom, if not practised in the classroom. One can see how, from this basis, a political attack could be conjured up by rumour and distortion.

The school was already subjected to pressures by the social make-up of its intake (see chapter 1). The three managers most concerned with the school at this time, Burnett, Gittings and Dewhurst, were all from the middle-class group. Dewhurst and Gittings were in many ways similar — both wives of journalists, both educated women unable to pursue careers because of young families, both new to school management.

On May 22nd these two met to discuss 'parental concern', and alleged bullying in the playground. Strangely, they took up these allegations with Burnett the next day, the very day of the first unofficial strike. Burnett, when asked at the inquiry to name the complaining parents, could only remember two besides Gittings and Dewhurst themselves, and one of these was Hercules.

Hercules, a close friend of Gittings, had returned in February, to find Ellis had dismissed her. She had later withdrawn her child on the grounds that he was not receiving a proper education; on May 24th these complaints were embodied in a letter to the school. As she had originally been the teacher in her child's class, the logic of her complaint is hard to follow. She thereafter appeared consistently in the Tyndale story as a critic of the school, though this consistency didn't extend to attendance at the inquiry to give the evidence she claimed to have against the school.

The sum of the allegations made to Burnett in May 1974 was that parents were worried, and that Ellis was rude to them when they tried to discuss matters with him. But Ellis had seen few parents in the first months of his headship. His complaint was that they did not come to him with their worries, but went instead to certain managers, who were setting themselves up as a channel of parental communication. Ellis was not prepared to act on second-hand information from unspecified sources. But why, if the professional parents were putting pressure on the school, did the working class parents not support it? Here we return to the political question, and the activities Walker now undertook.

Her paper on May 22nd, presented in the staffroom, was set for discussion on June 5th, after half-term, because some staff had been away on a school journey. But she was now extending her net further. She had consistently failed to carry the staff majority, and had no reason to suppose Ellis would take a unilateral decision in her favour. So before the meeting, some time between May 27th and 31st, she telephoned Burnett, and criticised the running of the school, with special reference to Ellis and McWhirter. Though Burnett came to Ellis on June 3rd with her worries about the direction in which the school was moving, she did not inform him of this phone call; neither did Walker. The precedent was set for the secret dealings that were to pollute the atmosphere of the school.

On June 3rd the Infant staff invited Rice to hear their complaints about the Juniors, and the next day, unknown to the Juniors, started recording these, even down to keeping as 'exhibits', stuck on card and labelled, individual stones allegedly thrown by children. June 11th loomed large on this list of Junior transgressions: yet on that day the school was closed because of a London allowance strike.

24

Where two schools share a building complaints are inevitable. The Infants' was well-established. Hart had battled to change its pattern in the late 1960s, a time when new departures were more acceptable and money available to back them. The Infants' had, moreover, been favoured in the immediate past by receiving more allowance than the Juniors, even though it had fewer children. As its future was at that time bound to that of the Juniors, no good could come of mutual recrimination. It is an open question why such a 'flourishing' establishment did not do all in its power to aid its neighbour that had a new head and comparatively new staff.

At the managers' meeting of June 3rd the atmosphere was cooler. Haddow made his report on the school journey. He suggested that in cases of limited grant availability, priority for school journey places should be based on economic need, not a system of random selection, since it was more important for the economically deprived to have one holiday than for the privileged to have an ILEA-sponsored trip in addition to their normal vacation. This provoked a strong response from manager Robin Mabey, who was to play an important part in the future of Tyndale. An economist and councillor for St Mary's Ward (in which Tyndale is situated); he was a prominent member of the South Islington Labour Party, and had once stood for parliamentary nomination there. He had also been chairman of governors in a local comprehensive. He said bluntly that Haddow's view would alienate the middle-classes from state education. He admitted to the inquiry that he saw Haddow's comment as a political statement. The fact that his own remark derived from his political thinking seems to have escaped him.

Gittings now took up the question of the 'falling roll' (the fall had been six, five from the 'split' class) and linked it with alleged bullying, instancing the Hercules child. (Hercules had not made a complaint about bullying.) Dewhurst then took up the question of alleged staff slackness. Ellis and Haddow were amazed that Burnett could permit such allegations without evidence or prior notice. Later, the 'bullying' charge was investigated by both Ellis and Hart, and found to be groundless. But the impression had been given to the managing body, most of whom had never visited the school, that things were not right in the Juniors.

Afterwards, Burnett suggested a private meeting between herself, Gittings, Dewhurst, Ellis and Haddow on June 7th, to discuss matters further. The two teachers agreed, in the hope of restoring good relations.

Gittings did not waste time. On June 5th and 6th she visited classrooms, unannounced. The first recipient of such a visit was McColgan, who had been at the school just over 4 weeks, and was still settling in. She had endured more than her fair share of pressure in the past, and was disquieted by questioning from a person she hardly knew. Gittings was 'collecting material' for the June 7th meeting. The next day she returned to check on standards in Green's class, specifically on behalf of one of her friends, Joan Chasin. By this time, Ellis had sought advice from the NUT, which was that managers should notify the head of their presence in the school. This information was not well received by Gittings. Relationships with managers started to sour.

On June 5th, Walker's paper was discussed at a staff meeting. The personal attacks, as well as the strident tone, were not a basis for fruitful discussion. You cannot expect people to listen if you call them 'buck-passer' (as Walker called Ellis in the document), or impugn the integrity of a colleague, as she had done to McWhirter. Her proposal to call unilaterally a parents' meeting was not well received, even by those, like Chowles, who might have had sympathy with her views. But parents were worried, she maintained. Which parents? Ellis had received no serious complaints. She, like the managers, would disclose no names. The staff suspected she was using alleged complaints to add strength to her efforts to change the direction of the school. When the majority went against her, it was plain she could no longer hope to influence policy by internal pressure.

The next day, Burnett telephoned Walker to find out what had happened at the staff meeting—an astonishing action on the part of a chairwoman of managers. At the inquiry Burnett said she did not consider the matter important enough to inform Ellis about it.

The June 7th teachers-managers meeting was lengthy, and pervaded by mutual suspicion. Gittings' visits had aroused the hostility of both Ellis and Haddow. Discussion ranged over the curriculum, rumours of bullying, alleged lack of supervision of children and staff lateness. The teachers were concerned about the way Gittings and Dewhurst seemed to abrogate the position of spokeswomen for parents, whose names were not disclosed. Ellis and Haddow were anxious to restore good relations, but felt that Gittings and Dewhurst were beginning to interfere in the internal

26

running of the school. Then Burnett, under pressure from Haddow, revealed her contacts with Walker, but not their content. Haddow tried to tell the managers about Walker's attitude and views, but they refused to listen. However, in order to accommodate them even further, Ellis finally agreed to discuss the curriculum again with Gittings and Dewhurst on June 13th.

Some managers, in evidence to the inquiry, seemed to suggest that Ellis was afflicted with paranoia, seeing conspiracies in every corner. But Burnett's dabbling with Walker was disconcerting, and any head who learns that his Chairwoman has been in covert communication with a part-time teacher who opposes him, is likely to feel he is not among friends. In the light of Walker's later actions, Burnett's secrecy assumed a sinister aspect and completely broke the trust a school should feel in its Chairwoman of managers.

Walker now stepped up her activity. She had drafted another document, which she took to Gittings on June 11th. This contained a fierce attack on certain kinds of modern educational practices, pointing out how these could lead to a revolutionary take-over of the country. Gittings discussed the paper and advised Walker to remove the political observations, as they would be 'counter-productive'. Walker claimed this document was for a staff meeting, though she shortly afterwards showed it to parents.

It was plain that the views of Ellis and Walker could not be reconciled. He therefore suggested that if she could not support school policy she should seek a post elsewhere. On June 13th the schoolkeeper, Gordon Campbell, reported to Ellis rumours of a petition in support of a teacher who was being sacked, and of an impending parents' meeting in the playground. When Ellis met Gittings and Dewhurst he put these matters to them, but they shrugged them off.

The same afternoon, however, Dewhurst came to summon Ellis and Haddow to such a meeting. Haddow was teaching, but Ellis went to speak to parents. The ubiquitous Gittings was present, with about a dozen parents. Though both managers claimed it was spontaneous, Ellis thought that the meeting was pre-arranged. It was certainly unpleasant, with some parents shouting; but Ellis spoke to them, and thought he had calmed them and allayed their anxieties.

A number of the parents at the meeting had had children in Walker's remedial groups, and were close contacts of hers. There were also the events of that evening. In support of the London allowance campaign the staff had been on strike on June 11th, and had given notice of doing so again on the 14th. They held a meeting to explain their action to parents. Every effort was made to get a good attendance, teachers even going to parents' homes. Ellis outlined the history of the London allowance, and a guest speaker, a parent from Hackney, told of the need to retain as many teachers as possible in London.

When discussion was thrown open, one parent, Christine McNamara, launched into an insulting tirade, calling Ellis 'a second-hand ragbag'. The strange thing about this outburst was that she did not know the person conducting the meeting was Ellis. But her child had been one of Walker's remedial readers, and she was friendly with Walker.

After this, the meeting became an acrimonious debate on the merits and demerits of unofficial action, until a number of vociferous parents tried to turn it into an investigation of the philosophy and methods of the school. Burnett and Mabey, although not parents, had come to the meeting. In his statement to the inquiry, Mabey made it clear he believed teachers were trying to use parents 'to further wider objectives'. When Ellis agreed to a further meeting to discuss education, it was suggested from the floor that the chairman of managers preside over this, and, naturally, Burnett, who was totally unknown to most parents, stepped forward to announce that she was chairwoman, and would be glad to be of service. By general vote it was decided that support for the London allowance be dependent on support for the school's policy.

There were two groups of vociferous parents at this meeting — one middle-class, the other working-class. As the latter left the hall, they were met by Walker, who had not attended the meeting. Although the staff did not know it, she went away with these parents to discuss the paper she had shown to Gittings.

On June 17th Burnett made it clear that the projected parents' meeting should be held before the next managers' meeting, scheduled for July 8th. The staff saw this as a contrivance on the part of certain managers to gain control over school policy by subjecting parents' meetings to managerial discussion. Ellis consulted Divisional Officer Hedley Wales, the senior local ILEA official, a veteran of many Islington conflicts. His view was that Ellis alone was responsible for calling the meeting.

The scene, meanwhile, was beginning to widen. Anne Page had been elected Islington representative to ILEA on May 21st—a speedy elevation for such a new councillor. Wife of a senior editor of the *Sunday Times*, she was a prominent Labour Party member in the St Peter's Ward, to which Burnett also belonged, and a managerial colleague of Mabey at Islington Green School. As early as mid-June, Burnett was expressing 'concern' about Tyndale to her. On June 26th, a meeting was held at County Hall for all North London managers. Burnett and Gittings asked questions and sought advice about the possibilities open when there was disagreement between managers and a head and about what control of curriculum could be exercised by managing bodies. Page also approached ILEA member Irene Chaplin, and subsequently telephoned ILEA Schools' Sub-committee Chairman and Labour Chief Whip, Harvey Hinds.

Within a fortnight of the June 13th meeting, Tyndale had been elevated to the highest levels of ILEA, not through the usual channels of administration and inspectorate, but through an exclusively Labour Party network. It seems a curiously rapid escalation of a case ostensibly concerned with a group of parents discontented with their children's education.

On June 27th Rice visited the Infants' to hear their complaints about the Juniors', whose teachers were ignorant of the matter. The staff now decided on a procedure for the forthcoming parents' meeting. Open evenings were to be held on July 2nd and 3rd. Here problems and complaints could be discussed between individual teachers and parents, and children's work would be on display. The main meeting, to be held on July 9th, was planned as a forum for the discussion of general ideas. In this way, matters could be kept calm, and some purposeful connection between parents and staff established.

On June 27th Gittings and Dewhurst put pressure on Burnett to change the date of the managers' meeting to July 15th. This was done, and all managers were invited to the parents' meeting by Wales. Haddow's letter of protest about the arbitrary change of date had no effect.

The Tyndale affair, having ascended the Labour Party ladder to Hinds, started back down again through the ILEA administrative pipe-line. In late June, Rice was asked by County Hall to make an inspection report.

Walker, on June 28th, telephoned Hart and asked permission to circulate her paper at the Infant Summer Fair the next day. This document had, after her discussion with Gittings and a few disgruntled parents, and much re-writing, reached its definitive form. At the inquiry, Walker at first stated that Gittings had suggested contact with Hart, but, after Gittings disagreed with this, Walker changed her evidence and said that another parent (who did not come to give evidence) had made the suggestion. In any case, Hart refused permission, and informed Ellis on July 3rd.

In early July two parents, both from the Infants', wrote letters of complaint to Divisional Office about the Juniors'. Barbara Goward, who had never been in the Juniors' nor met any of its staff, complained of the 'very left-wing views' of some teachers, and said they were only interested in working-class and deprived children. This was the first occasion when politics was brought publicly into the Tyndale affair, and when the idea was put forward that the school's philosophy was anti-middle-class. Goward's complaints illustrate the kind of rumour circulating about the Tyndale philosophy in July 1974. She never gave evidence at the inquiry, so her sources of information remain a matter of conjecture.

The parents' evenings of July 2nd and 3rd were poorly attended, and there was no criticism of the school's policy or practice. But on the first evening a parent handed Ellis a document, brought to his home by a Junior teacher who did not introduce herself. It was entitled 'A criticism of the 'free choice' method of education based on total children's rights, as at William Tyndale Junior School'. This was Walker's paper in its final form, henceforth known to Tyndale staff as the 'Black Paper'. It contained a fierce attack on the kind of methods — 'free choice' and 'total children's rights' — that Walker said were practised in the school, but which were not. It expressed a strong anti-progressive ideology, which, as parent John Newman said, 'would, if adopted, put the clock back fifty years'. It played on the fears of working-class parents for their children's future, their salvation through education.

If Walker was writing things like this, what was she saying to parents? The answer was not long in coming. Shortly afterwards, two parents, Alice Frankel and Erica Jones, brought copies of the same papers to Ellis. They alleged that Walker had told them that Haddow was a 'Trotskyite' and was indoctrinating the children. From what they said, it was plain that she was canvassing parents, and attributing difficulties of the school to political motivation on the part of staff.

Through information from another parent, it seemed a local politician was stating that McColgan was a trouble-maker and a Communist. He had offered to write a denunciation of McColgan, to be read out to parents on July 9th. Yet another parent, Amanda Ascott, then reported that the parents' meeting was going to be used to attack Haddow. The 'charge' against him was that he had been dismissed from his last school for being too 'revolutionary'. (At the inquiry the headmistress of his previous school gave evidence of the value of his work, and the high regard in which she held him.)

On July 4th, Walker placed two copies of her paper on Ellis's desk. He hesitated to discuss the matter, since he felt certain anything he said would be misrepresented. Instead, he tabulated a careful set of written questions to her, seeking hard facts about its drafting and distribution. She answered evasively. He wrote out a further set, which she declined to answer. By now, both Haddow and McColgan had written letters of complaint concerning the allegations being made about them. These were sent immediately to Divisional Office, where no action was taken—a treatment not to be given to letters of complaint *against* Ellis and his supporters. By the time of the inquiry, the teachers' letters had disappeared. Haddow also complained in writing to Walker about what she had said to parents. She never replied.

Since it appeared the July 9th meeting was to be used for illegitimate ends, the staff who felt threatened consulted the NUT, which advised them not to attend. They were now in a quandary. Ellis had called the meeting; so he had to go. And there was little choice for his supporters. Non-attendance would undoubtedly be construed as non-cooperation with parents and would leave Ellis unsupported. Attendance risked attack. They finally decided to go. As it transpired, they got the worst of both worlds.

Meanwhile, activated by the NUT, high-level consultations took place at County Hall, and Rice was instructed to attend the meeting. Since both Ellis and Burnett had been anxious for an independent record, an experienced official was to be sent from Divisional Office.

On July 7th parent Anna Sullivan, who supported the staff, held a meeting in her home to discuss Walker's document. Haddow was invited, but refused on the grounds that it would be improper for him to discuss another teacher's views with parents. Gittings and Dewhurst, however, invited themselves, and made it clear to the parents that they disliked Ellis's conduct of the school.

About this time, Walker was in contact with Rhodes Boyson, Conservative MP for Brent North. Her letter is not extant, but he replied on July 10th, asking about the parents' meeting. 'More power to you', he said, 'I believe that we can turn the tide'. He signed off with 'very fondest regards'—hardly the words of a person writing to a casual correspondent (Walker later claimed that her links with Boyson were only of the most tenuous kind). He found the contents of Walker's letter 'fascinating'. Something of them can be gauged from his book *Crisis in Education*, where he mentions a version of the 'tigers' quote, and links it with the reading problem at the school. He omits to mention, however, that Walker had been the remedial teacher for five years, and that the reading problem had existed before the arrival of the staff whom Walker opposed.

Further disquieting information came through Dewhurst. It was being alleged that the staff were a political cell, and that political meetings were being held in the school. Although not revealed until the inquiry, Dewhurst's informant was Walker. They were in personal and telephone contact during this period.

A decision was now taken that Ellis should speak for all staff at the parents' meeting. A brief paper, which all staff including Walker agreed to, was prepared as a guide for discussion. It contained five simple educational points, intended as pegs on which questions could be hung. It was intended that the filling out and detailing of this sketch should be a useful way of communicating philosophy and practice without the atmosphere becoming heated. Ellis and Burnett placed papers on chairs before the meeting began. Unknown to them, Walker later placed her own document on top.

She had prepared her ground well. Together with Eileen Horsman, parent and ancillary helper, she secretly circulated copies to a number of parents in their homes, some of whom thought it was an official document. Some addresses had been obtained by going through the school files. Others, of Infant parents, had obviously been supplied by another contact. It had therefore been suggested to some parents, in the week before the meeting, that there was something drastically wrong with the school.

The July 9th meeting was a fiasco, in full view of parents, potential parents, the inspector and half the managing body. In parts it resembled one of those stormy political affairs, where a small group are allowed to harass a speaker into silence.

Walker, uninhibited by the presence of Rice, intervened at an early stage. She was to claim later that her paper was meant as a guide for discussion, to prevent matters becoming acrimonious. But now she did not speak about its contents, nor attempt any debate on the points raised in the staff documents. Instead she launched into a long emotional speech on an entirely personal level, saying Ellis's policies were 'sheer madness', that he gave no help to younger members of staff, that one teacher had his ear 'almost exclusively' and was advocating 'free choice' education throughout the school, that Ellis was attempting to get her out.

All this raised the temperature to a level where cool, lucid discussion was impossible. In trying to reply, Ellis was heckled by her supporters. Burnett had prevented the denunciations by firmly quashing an attempt on the part of the Walker faction to get motions admitted to the meeting. But the managers did not need motions here, they could pass their own resolution later.

Burnett's role here is open to question. The teachers were already suspicious because of her contacts with Walker, and became even more so when she allowed Walker's tirade to continue. Walker believed the Chair had shielded Ellis unfairly, although it did not seem like that to him: he felt he had been thrown to the wolves. When parent Jones indignantly objected to Walker's coming to her home and discussing Haddow's politics, she was cut short by Burnett, who insisted that politics could not be discussed.

One is reminded of Gittings' advice to Walker to delete the political references in her original document, as these might be 'counter-productive'. To raise politics overtly as a method of attacking teachers is an unsubtle tactic. It is less publicly contentious to scapegoat them for their educational practice or accuse them of incompetence, on the principle that if you do not like a teacher's politics, you pretend you have more acceptable reasons for your attack. Had Jones been allowed to continue, she might have discredited Walker's attack by revealing its political basis.

Feeling continued to run high. Parents spoke for and against the school. Newman came out strongly against Walker. Rice at last rose to make a contribution, calling for support. But his stance, too, had been curious. He had not obviously aligned himself with Ellis by sitting on the platform with him, but sat in the audience instead. He had not intervened during Walker's attack. It had therefore not been made crystal clear to the parents that ILEA's representative was with

Ellis and his supporters and against Walker. He appeared rather as one observing Ellis, to see how he performed.

The hostile overtone was to dictate the response of the teachers. Although Haddow had seen individual parents and discussed his work with them at open evenings, questions were being asked which were obviously directed at his educational practice. The 'free choice' part of Walker's paper was an overt attack on his options system. When a parent, Diana Erwin, mentioned Haddow by name, it seemed, in the fraught atmosphere, that 'denunciation' time had come. Haddow, McWhirter, Richards, McColgan and Green rose and left, something later described by a subsequent chairman of managers, Brian Tennant, as a 'political act'. Uproar followed as Ellis tried to explain the reasons for their action

Things had calmed down a little by the time the proceedings closed, but the damage had been done. Managers and parents had seen the head savagely attacked by Walker. Few knew of the events that led up to this, and many then made the decision to withdraw their children, even some who might well have supported the school's future policies. Sheila Best, for example, agreed with progressive education and gave evidence for the teachers at the inquiry. But, after July 9th, she foresaw conflict, did not want her children involved, and removed them.

The meeting was used by Walker and others to force a change in the future direction of the school. Its real effect was to begin the slow process of destruction. In a later letter to Boyson, Walker was to affirm her 'major part in the parents' revolt' and the fact that 'the managers are alerted'. It was certain now that more managers would take a long critical look at the school. The inquisitorial tone in managers' meetings, the lightning visits, the demands for the curriculum, the monitoring of standards—were about to begin.

The majority of staff were furious about Walker's conduct. Rice counselled calm, and asked for the matter to be left to him. Walker was unabashed. She sent Ellis, Rice and Burnett a long critique of the five points of staff policy presented at the meeting. The staff were astounded. Their reaction was that Walker had now proceeded from thinking she was headmistress to thinking she was inspector. The paper was not even acknowledged: there seemed no possibility of reconciling the differences between her and the majority of her colleagues.

Term ended on July 19th, to the relief of the exhausted
34

teachers. The last days saw a great deal of secret activity, some of which overlapped into the summer holiday and the following term (see Chapter 5).

Rice had been at work providing the information requested by Hinds. His report was sent to County Hall on July 11th, but went astray in the pipeline, and was never received by Hinds. This document was the first 'professional' assessment of the school since Buxton's paean of praise of November 1973.

Rice appeared to believe the introduction of 'cooperative teaching' had caused indiscipline among children. But there *was* no cooperative teaching at this time: the children were still in a class-teaching system. Certainly the school was in a transitional phase and under considerable pressure, both from stresses inherent in an inner-city school with a comparatively new head and staff, and from outside harassment. But Rice ignored all this, and found the usual scape-goats, the teachers.

He asserts that the staff are 'relatively inexperienced'. Here we are in the realms of fantasy, since the total experience of Ellis and his eight full-time teachers was over sixty years — amazingly high for a London school at that time. Ellis is said to be 'too much influenced by different points of view among his staff, some of whom have actively opposed him': a criticism of the democratic decision-making process.

He also states his concern that 'standards of both behaviour and attainment have fallen'. How did he know they had? He had first seen the school only three months previously, as a newcomer to Inner London. He had done no attainment tests, nor asked for the results of any done by teachers. Nor had he seen Buxton's report which mentions 'high standards'. By what yardstick, then, is he judging?

The staff were not told of this report.

Rice made three proposals for the future: his attendance at a staff meeting the following term, provision of a large sum of money for both Juniors' and Infants', and the creation of a psycho-therapy unit in the Juniors'. The second proposal is curious, since only the Juniors' was under pressure. The well-established Infants' would, nevertheless, get just as much extra money: there was clearly to be no erosion of differentials here. On the third proposal, Ellis had already put to Rice the idea of a 'sanctuary' for disturbed children, and as early as March had suggested the clearing of a redundant cloakroom for this purpose.

On the day he apparently completed his report, July 8th, Rice was visited by Chowles, who was unhappy about the 'team-teaching' in the school, which as has been noted, did not exist. Rice reminded her she was deputy head, and told her to put her point of view.

The role of Chowles in the Tyndale affair has never been very clear. Her acting headship in 1973 had been an exhausting affair. In early 1974 she had been tired and ill, tended to retreat into her own class, and shown a lack of sympathy with the progressive educational philosophies expressed in discussion. Ellis had turned more and more towards Haddow as de facto deputy, and this had caused resentment. As a teacher inclined to structured methods, she was philosophically and politically more in tune with Walker than anyone else. Working-class Islington has a village-like atmosphere and takes time to get used to 'new faces'. Many parents tended to trust and turn to the old teachers like Chowles and Walker.

The managers' meeting was due on the evening of July 15th. That morning Burnett asked for material from the school files — letters that Haddow had sent out to parents. Ellis refused, and later went to Divisional Office to complain. Burnett was already there, discussing the school with Rice. The officials anxiously kept Ellis and Burnett apart, though why they should not meet is not clear. Ellis made it plain that he did not consider it the business of managers to carry out private investigations into the work of individual teachers.

Rice and Wales were at the managers' meeting. The official note of the parents' meeting was not there. For both teachers and managers this was disturbing. Where was the note? Not in a fit form to be presented, said Wales. Others had managed to take coherent notes, but this document remained buried until the inquiry. In view of the fact that there might well be serious repercussions from Walker's actions, the suppression of the official record took on a sinister aspect, and was to condition Ellis's thinking when he had to consider whether to pursue a complaint against her. It looked like a 'cover-up' of the fact that Walker had attacked Ellis.

During discussion Gittings disclosed her contact with Walker, and her knowledge of the 'Black Paper' in draft. Dewhurst attempted to make a statement, but was ruled out by the Chair. Walker's actions could not be discussed, since the case had now been referred to County Hall. This new knowledge about Gittings, coming after Walker's performance on July 9th and her contacts with Burnett, confirmed the teachers' suspicion that she had been involved with these managers in an attempt to overturn school policy.

There was talk about the formation of a parent-teacher association. These are normally institutions concerned with fund-raising but what seemed envisaged here was a powerful, policy-making body dominated by those who claimed to represent the parental view—a barrier between teachers and parents rather than a bridge. Ellis and Haddow resisted this, and were supported by Rice.

The managers expressed concern over the curriculum, and Ellis promised a statement the following term, although this was not a usual practice. He insisted both schools receive the same treatment, and Hart promised to outline her curriculum.

Those teachers who had left the parents' meeting had presented a letter of explanation to the managers. They in turn now passed a watery resolution, regretting the fact that things had occurred on July 9th that might have been construed as attacks. But no construction needed to be put on Walker's actions; they had been glaringly obvious.

Even after this meeting, some people could not wait until the next term. Gittings and Dewhurst, who had already decided to remove their children, found a new ally in the Vice-Chairwoman of managers. Valerie Fairweather was the wife of a Labour Party Alderman, and chairwoman of managers in a neighbouring school. She, like Gittings and Dewhurst, was one of the new Islington middle-class, and had children in the Infants. They discussed the Juniors' on July 16th, not with Ellis, but with Hart. These managers wanted further consultations with Rice, although he had already put to the whole body his proposals for extra money for both schools. Fairweather contacted him, but he insisted on the presence of Burnett. A more proper procedure would have been to invite Ellis, but this was not done. The meeting was fixed for July 23rd at Divisional Office.

It was strongly argued by some parties in the inquiry that those criticising the school during this period had every justification, since there was a sudden and serious decline in its efficiency. There is, however, no evidence of any deterioration in academic standards, and much of the parental 'evidence' about children's lack of achievement consisted of people repeating what they had been told by others.

The year had seen many changes of personnel, including two different heads; some classes, due to these changes and staff absences, had had a number of teachers in a short period. Staff in London were used to dealing with such difficulties and were capable of dealing with them effectively. The Tyndale staff, however, had been attacked from the outside, and internally sabotaged.

Two teachers were leaving that summer. The remainder devoted a great deal of time to discussing future organisation. It had been decided that one of the school's main needs was a teacher with responsibility for children with behavioural and learning problems. On July 18th the managers appointed David Austin. He was an experienced teacher who had previously worked in a team-teaching system. He had visited the school before his application, and was in sympathy with the educational views of the majority of staff. The same applied to Steve Felton, a secondary school teacher who wished to work with Juniors, but was seeking a 'progressive' establishment. He joined the staff in September.

So for 1974-5 there was the prospect of a united staff with an agreed policy, working within an organisation they had chosen and planned. But how many children would they have to teach? Sixty-two were leaving for secondary school, only forty-nine were due for transfer from the Infants'. Add to that the natural wastage in an area of falling rolls, and decline was inevitable. Nobody knew how many would be removed or not transferred as a result of the events of the summer term.

One thing was certain. Never again would the teachers permit the semblance of an attack on them without a strong reaction. They wanted to be left in peace, to work through their educational plans, to liaise with parents without interference, and provide for the children a relevant educational experience. But events were already in motion that would make the following year a gradual climb towards open conflict.

Chapter 4
A Conflict of Ideas

By the time of the inquiry (October 1975), the staff had no shortage of opponents. But to indicate a common political or educational position among these groups would be to over-simplify. The attack on the school began not in 1975, but in May 1974. By July it was obvious that open discussion, designed to produce a coherent direction for development, had brought about a savage ideological conflict. With the arrival of Austin and Felton in September 1974, Walker's isolation was almost complete, except for the support of Chowles; thereafter the school proceeded in a new direction. It is due to Walker's importance as a catalyst in the conflict building up around the school that an analysis must be made of the political and educational views that she placed in opposition to the emerging philosophy of the majority of her colleagues.

Through the media an image has been presented of Walker as a concerned teacher worried about a particular situation in a school of unparalleled frightfulness; a woman determined to help parents who could not speak for themselves to secure an acceptable education for their children. At the inquiry she put herself forward as neither 'traditional' nor 'progressive', but simply concerned about the children's welfare. No one has ever denied that she was concerned.

It was equally clear, however, that despite her animated outbursts, her habit of going off at tangents in argument and dragging in personal details, Walker's opinions and reactions were formed by a political/educational ideology of long standing, to which she was deeply committed, and which encompassed a 'global' view of schools and society.

Although the staff labelled her document of July 1974 the 'Black Paper', Walker claimed in the inquiry she knew little of the theories of Black Paper writers and their sympathisers. Yet she was in constant, cordial contact with a leading Black Paper figure, Boyson, from the time she made her first attacks on her colleagues' philosophy until the beginning of the inquiry. The documents she produced at the inquiry totalling 8,000 words, are an accurate summary of many aspects of Black Paper theory.

Black Paper theory holds that 'schools are for schooling', and opposes any idea that they should concern themselves with social development as a matter of priority. Schooling is envisaged as academic, highly structured, carried on in an authoritarian context, designed to produce people able to do the jobs western capitalist society requires even better than their predecessors, thus ensuring its continued and vigorous expansion. Education is to be based on elitism and competition. Examinations and tests assume a vital importance, since everything must be quantified and measured. Central control of schools is advocated through a series of national tests of ability at specific ages. Boyson himself, by his support of a 'voucher' system (which Walker thoroughly endorsed), has advocated an extension of market-place economics into education.

Such theories are at odds with those of 'progressive' education, in its ideal sense. The Black Paper writers identify progressives as their enemies, and seek to discredit their theories and practice. To do this they, quite correctly, point out that there is a crisis in education, and, quite incorrectly, blame it on the spread of 'progressive' ideas, picturing a school system swept into chaos by 'millenarian fantasies'. But this crisis in education is only a reflection of a more general malaise in society.

The Tyndale teachers would have agreed there was a crisis; authorities like ILEA, and 'progressive' bodies like the Tyndale managers, will admit nothing of the kind. They seek other explanations for the ills of schools; and the natural target for criticism is the teacher. This plays straight into the hands of people like Walker. Parents sense there is a crisis; the Walkers of the world have seized the initiative in explaining it to them, while education authorities are busy with public relations exercises designed to prove nothing is wrong. This provides much of the explanation of an important paradox — many believe that Black Paper theory is essentially against the interest of working-class parents and children, yet it is primarily to the working class that it appeals, because it appears to provide an explanation in an area where no one else is giving reasons.

Why, at the inquiry, did inspectors of 'liberal' ILEA, like Pape and Rice, find so much to commend in the collected works of Walker? The Tyndale affair had put ILEA in a ludicrous position, since many were using the school to discredit them in a general sense. So it was necessary to present Tyndale as untypical of ILEA schools, and they used the most convenient educational analysis — Walker's. She, of course, believed Tyndale to be an example of a general malaise. Thus the same arguments were being used to justify mutually exclusive propositions, illustrating the contradictory position 'liberal' educationalists are forced to take up when the crunch comes.

All education theories have a political basis, and those of the Black Papers are no exception. Richard Lynn, for example, has argued that western capitalism provides the best form of society known to man. 'It has its internal enemies,' he writes, 'such as millenarians, also its enemies in the communist bloc and Third World, who would like to see it destroyed. If it is to be preserved, we need to maintain both our economic and our military strength. For this, the population, and especially the country's leadership, need to be imbued with the competitive spirit and the ideal of excellence.'

Those who advocate anti-Black Paper theories of education are seen as enemies of society, and are linked with communism. An echo of this is found in Walker's views. Yet Lynn is not just arguing for the status quo, but for strengthening it in a certain direction. Politically, Black Paper theory demands that education be the tool that re-invigorates western capitalism and creates a society based on authoritarianism, elitism, a leadership principle, and the competition of man against man. It is a dynamic creed masquerading as an attempt to preserve the established order.

It claims to attempt to re-establish all that was good in the past, old values lost through the invasion of our society by 'trendy' ideas on morals and education. Boyson himself has extolled the virtues of Victorian England; Walker laid great store by 'time-honoured' methods. A familiar charge directed against progressive theorists is that they are 'millenarian', working to establish a future golden age, which is seen by Black Paper supporters as mere fantasy. But they are indulging in an even bigger fantasy — the forcible resurrection of the past in order to shape the future. Nostalgia, like patriotism, is surely not enough: though their ideas are not without appeal in our fractured society.

To represent the Tyndale conflict as, in part, a battle between progressive and traditional education is an over-simplification. If Walker's views were 'radical', in its original sense of wishing to make 'root' changes, so were those of her many opponents on the staff. As she was not just 'traditional', they were not just 'progressive'. Both sides found much to criticise in the 'liberal' educational view adopted by the ILEA image-makers and the Tyndale managers. The staff were attacked by those who thought themselves progressive, and the managers accused them of bringing progressive education into disrepute.

What was this philosophy that provoked such wrath? Any statement represents the consensus of up to eight individual views, constantly modified by cross-fertilization of ideas, re-appraised in the light of problems, of practices that succeeded or failed, and subjected to perpetual re-shaping in open discussion. Individuals within the group made divers emphases; differing areas assumed importance at various times.

Much might appear to be embraced by the term 'progressive', if that word itself had not become virtually meaningless. Inspector Pape, asked to define the concept for the inquiry, said, 'Moving forward slowly'. This, besides being a formula for doing nothing, is an effective method of not defining it at all. The Tyndale staff were aware of the contradictions in much so-called progressive education, how it is often simply traditional education in disguise, the means more indirect, the manner more showy, the ends exactly the same. They knew that many forward-looking ideas thrown out in the balmy air of the 1960s were in the process of freezing to death in the cold, uncomforting climate of today, that many teachers who had spoken so resoundingly then of 'fluidity in the

42

curriculum' and 'responding to kids' were now retreating into
cautious mutterings about 'structure' and 'maintaining standards'.
In many ways, the staff were seeking to carry through to a logical
conclusion many ideas that had seemed exciting in the post-Plowden
era, while breaking through the progressive contradictions, by
reaching out to more radical perspectives and methods.

Among the documents relating to the first inspection report on
Tyndale in September 1975 is a memorandum by Inspector Norman
Geddes. It is not a report, but a description of his experiences with
the class he had to teach when the teachers were on strike. He
performs the unique act of inspecting his own teaching, and finding
it good. He battles against his rebellious pupils, and gains control.
The most striking phrase he uses is: 'by the second afternoon there
was a definite impression that sir was winning'. This unmasks a set of
assumptions about the teacher's role. How does 'sir' see himself?
And if 'sir' is winning, whom is he fighting; and, above all, who is
losing?

Schools have always been concerned with social control. In
many it is an amalgam of obsessions — with uniforms, length of hair,
'bad' language, religious sanctions and petty secular rules. Schooling
is a matter of conditioning those schooled into the acceptance of
such modes of thinking and acting as society deems proper. The
teacher, as part of the apparatus of control, has assumed the roles of
law-giver, moraliser, indoctrinator, communicator of the acceptable
views and taboos of the tribe — a strict father or mother backed up
by the system as long as those in control think the job is being done
effectively.

The ferment of ideas in the 1960s threatened to crack this
mould. Active rather than passive learning became the accepted
theory; subject divisions were blurred; greater emphasis was placed
on human relationships and social development; classrooms were
arranged as informal workshops, no longer as schooling boxes
dominated by a centrally important teacher. The means and much of
the content of schooling was changed — though not overnight, nor in
many schools.

Content and method have a great influence on the role of the
teacher. It is more difficult to adopt a dominating stance in an
informal classroom, or to assume an obvious controlling and
conditioning position where pupils' views are thought to be
important. Had teachers taken the new methods to their logical

conclusion, and questioned the ends to which they were educating as they were now questioning the means, a change in the teacher's role might have taken place.

But the institution of school places teachers and taught in a false position towards each other. In addition, new methods created tensions between schools and working-class parents, as traditional methods had done with middle-class parents. It is impossible, in a society of increasing ethical disarray, to construct an ordered educational system agreed and understood by all. Working-class parents, a majority of the state system's clientele, became disturbed as their children's schools ceased to resemble their own homes, and became more like middle-class ones. Although teachers were trying to work in a fresh way, their results were still subjected to the old academic criteria of judgment: a 'liberal' Authority like ILEA, for example, tests all its children at 11 in English, Maths and Verbal Reasoning.

Under these pressures, most teachers adjusted and compromised. They bought the room to pursue a 'modern style' by a re-assertion of their role in a fresh, but only slightly amended, form. They have been led, for instance, into claims that their methods achieve what formal education sets out to do, only better and for more children. In such a school, unashamed coercion is no longer fashionable. Manipulation, more suited to indirect methods, has been substituted. Sir, as usual, is winning, and the children are still in their proper place, under firm control.

The teacher, who had been a strict parent, now becomes the occasionally severe aunt or uncle. Many have remarked on how much more strenuous such teaching is. This is quite understandable: being crafty all day is a tiring business. The real motives of schooling and the controlling role of the teacher have been gently evaded. The contradictions have been papered over with triple-mounted pictures and production-line creative writing. This moribund prettiness, devoid of all motive except the transference of middle-class values to working-class children, has been embraced by many schools, especially those with a strong middle-class parental element.

The Tyndale staff were trying to break through these contradictions when their efforts were smothered. In April 1975 Haddow attacked, in a staff discussion paper, 'the late 1960s style of informal progressive repression', and was to advocate the abolition of 'pointless structures', and the introduction of more

44

egalitarian systems for staff and children. The philosophy emerged slowly; many of the more radical ideas were still in the discussion stage, even then.

This philosophy was democratic, egalitarian and non-sexist; it was concerned with children's social development, with their individual needs and achievements; it was geared to activity, not passivity; made no false distinctions between 'work' and 'play'; rejected arbitary standards of attainment and behaviour; asserted the necessity for a wide range of choices, the involvement of children in their own community, and exercise of positive discrimination towards the disadvantaged; and encouraged children to think for themselves, and gain the confidence to dominate material presented to them. Children were encouraged to ask questions, not conditioned to obey orders, as Ellis emphasized at the inquiry. Maybe this was why 'sir' had such a hard time winning when the inspectors took over the school in September 1975?

Modern educationalists lay great emphasis on human relationships in school. But that institution fractures any real personal contact between teachers and children, through its compulsory nature, the expectations of it fed into children, and the role that adults are forced to adopt. Tyndale teachers sought to diminish the role-distance between them and their children, to a point where each could be seen to have something of value to offer the other on an equal level. They were to be continually frustrated in this, not only by outside interference but the nature of school itself, which demands forms of social control. They nevertheless believed, and tried to carry into practice, that individuals should be allowed to work out their frustrations, as long as this was not at somebody else's expense. They held that 'discipline' should come from within, and be based on consideration for others, not on a set of outdated moral precepts or crude rewards and punishments. They asserted, above all, that children had basic human rights, and were not an inferior species to be dragged out of its ignorance by well-meaning adults called teachers.

Behaviour that was either physically dangerous or emotionally damaging to others was not condoned but the conduct of children was seen as part of their emotional development, and was not treated in a moralising way. An attempt was made to integrate all kinds of behaviour into the life of the school, not to reject or accept on the bald terms of 'good' and 'bad'.

One of the important aspects of this philosophy related to children suffering social deprivation and lack of self-confidence, casualties that inner-city stress is producing in ever-increasing measure. In most schools emphasis is laid on 'pushing' the 'bright' child, and merely coping with those who show problems. The latter are referred for special classes, or accommodated in separate units within the school—a kind of 'dustbin' policy. Tyndale chose to reverse this. Plentiful activities were provided for the highly motivated children, but a large part of the staff's effort was directed towards the deprived group. The staff saw certain needs as more pressing than others, and set out to cater for them.

In the curriculum statement presented to the managers in October 1974, it was affirmed: 'That in a democratic society a wide range of choices and activities is essential, and that this should be reflected in that society's schools.' To this end, options systems were a prominent feature at Tyndale. Haddow ran one in his own class from March to July 1974. From September 1974 until July 1975, options were an important facet of team-teaching; the system would have been extended to the whole school the following year.

There is a tendency in schools to differentiate between 'work' and 'play', as if these were mutually exclusive. 'Work' is seen as tedious but necessary, on the basis that things which are boring and painful are morally good for children, as well as conditioning them for the wearisome and frustrating lives they are going to lead. The Tyndale teachers rejected this. They believed that 'work' and 'play' were indivisible activities, that formal skills could be learned through games, practical equipment and indirect methods. Knowing how to play was seen as a valuable skill; education was not seen as a process of producing young people to fit into convenient industrial niches. Leisure, and being able to use it, was vitally important.

The validity of experience for its own sake was stressed, running counter to the idea that visits and other activities must be incorporated into an academic framework. The fact that they are going to be forced, or cajoled, into academicism after an interesting activity often spoils children's immediate enjoyment, which would seem to defeat the primary purpose of the event. To the Tyndale staff the important thing was children being at the zoo, watching a great national event on television, or climbing a high tower, and relishing the experience both at the time and afterwards—and not just the written evidence of having done it, which is often more for the benefit of visitors and inspectors.

In all the school's activities, co-operation instead of competition was essential. This meant a view of Tyndale as an entity, not disparate groups and individuals. The staff meeting was the first attempt to embody this belief, and the co-operative projects of 1974 and 1975 carried it on. Children were encouraged to work together, not against each other to see who was 'top'; the age divisions in which they are usually grouped were broken up. Teachers came to see themselves as a team, not individuals competing to prove to an all powerful head that one was better than another. Attempts were made to widen this view by forming links with the surrounding community and securing co-operation of parents.

One of the persistent myths about a school working with an indirect teaching style based on options and human values is that the children are allowed to 'do as they like'. Yet the nature of the institution, the limitations of human and physical resources, mean choice and fluidity are at some point circumscribed. The building provides limits which are absolute, however one may seek to extend the frontiers. Factors of physical safety provide further boundaries. Choices of activity are restricted by the number of adults available, and the range of usable materials. There are more forms of limitation than areas of choice, even in the most 'liberal' institution.

Holding the views that she did, Walker was bound to oppose the Tyndale philosophy. It was a system in embryo she attacked in mid-1974: in attacking 'total children's rights' and 'free choice' she therefore opposed something which, in practical terms, did not exist, playing on the anxieties of working-class parents, and believing, rightly or wrongly, that some of the managers supported her. The circumstances and tactics of her opposition are as important as its content.

She had a history of opposition to modern teaching methods. She had attacked Hart's Infant School, and at least one former Junior teacher. Drafts of documents produced at the inquiry indicated a discontent pre-dating the arrival of most of the teachers she found so unsatisfactory in summer 1974.

Her May 22nd document was not an indication she had suddenly seen the light, but the first publication of views long ruminated over. She was at this time exceptionally busy in drafting papers about the school, but, since she rapidly took up underground methods of opposition, hardly any of these came to the notice of the staff until the inquiry.

It would be tempting, in analysing Walker's documents, to try to 'prove' the falsity of her premises, the illogicality of her argument, and the fatuity of her conclusions. Certainly there are minor areas in her philosophy that are suspect, and some confusion in the development of her arguments. But her views are a logical consequence of her philosophy of life, the way she saw human nature, children and social relationships. The conflict with her colleagues was one of philosophies of life and political outlook. It was almost on a metaphysical plane, with deep, irreconcilable conviction on both sides. It is no more possible to demonstrate, in an absolute sense, that Walker was wrong in her views than it is to show that the majority of her colleagues were wrong.

The May 22nd document, despite its confusions and personal rancour, indicates some of Walker's convictions. It features a swingeing attack on 'psychological' approaches to teaching, and on psychology in general. These, Walker, alleges, are fads emanating from the USA (a common Black Paper assertion), and have taken over the school, to the detriment of the children's interests.

Walker takes the view of children closely related to that of the Victorian era, when they were seen as adults writ small, with the devil still in them, and only of value insofar as they could be filled with goodness and discipline by adults. She writes of 'the unreasonableness and immaturity in which they are locked', and quotes with approval a parent stating that 'all children are basically inclined to be lazy'. She spoke at the inquiry of children left 'in their own ignorance'.

Children, then, are by nature in need of redemption. Who are to be the redeemers? Walker's answer is the parents and teachers. Yet in her writings she is careful not to criticize parents. They seem to be endowed with a natural instinct for coping with children, and are beyond reproach. The home is the fountain of goodness.

The teacher's function is to guide the children through various sequential stages, of which Junior School is only one, so that they can 'reap the benefits available' — the ability to earn a living for themselves or the ultimate reward of 'University life'. School is therefore to be run on arbitrary standards. Walker talks of children 'falling behind' or 'catching up'. Junior School is almost entirely a preparation for secondary: 'You feel no responsibility for the next stage in our children's education, even though you are ostensibly preparing them for this.'

If children are recalcitrant, Walker sees no problem. 'Time-honoured methods of reward and punishment' must be applied; we must not treat 'naughty' children as 'psychological cases'. Walker attributes a lot of bad behaviour to lack of attainment: solve the academic problem and the child is reformed. 'Once he is making good progress in reading and catching up with his peers, so the social/behavioural problem evaporates.' This discounts the home influence, and assumes academic learning is a priority with most children. Yet there is no evidence that literacy is a solution to social problems. Again, the problem is laid at the door of the school.

Walker often attributes to teachers views they do not hold. Ellis is said not to believe in literacy, on the basis of a joke he told in the staffroom. This tactic ran through all Walker's later communications, both open and secret. Most significant, however, is the following: 'Children are being *seduced* [her emphasis] to behave in ways which are detrimental to them.' This was the first indication that Walker saw a grand and sinister design in the teachers' emerging philosophy. The 'Black Paper' of early July took up many of these themes, and developed them further. It is a cooler and more lucid document than that of May. On its own terms, it is a cogent and powerful argument for a certain kind of education, an ideal discussion paper for staff-room or university education departments. But this was not the purpose it was put to. It was never brought to the staff for discussion, but distributed to parents. It was, however, produced with the knowledge of at least two of the school's ancillary helpers, and at least one of the school's managers. It originally contained an overt political section. Its circulation coincided with a period when Walker was in contact with Boyson, when she was making political allegations about her colleagues. It was produced when Ellis had only been in post a few months, and shortly after McColgan's appointment.

The nature of the paper also changes. A title was added: 'A criticism of the Free Choice method of education based on Total Children's Rights as at William Tyndale Junior School.' This, with changes in wording, transformed a general philosophical statement into an attack on a particular school—the setting up and knocking down of an Aunt Sally that did not exist. A paragraph was added beginning 'We parents . . .', thus suggesting, quite falsely, that the views were those of a substantial body of parents. Yet there was no evidence at the inquiry that any parent apart from Gittings influenced the writing of the paper.

The paper ignores the fact that 'free choice' and 'total children's rights' can never exist. It starts with the assumption they can, and actually did exist at Tyndale. It then lists the disadvantages of such a system—disorganisation, lack of learning incentives, unhappiness of children, behavioural problems, divisions between school and home.

This last is revealing : 'It divides children from parents and parental control and home discipline. It is the common experience of parents that their children become "difficult" at home, more rebellious even to the point of unreasonableness.' No mention is made of other factors that disorientate and confuse children, including the home itself. The fact that children spend their formative years in the home, and even when they come to school, only pass a small proportion of their lives there, is ignored. This is a seductive argument for parents struggling to make sense of our confused society, and the behaviour of their children. It provides a ready scapegoat for all ills—the school and its teachers.

Walker did not attempt on July 9th to discuss matters arising from her paper: she simply used it as a springboard for a direct attack on Ellis, and an indirect one on Haddow. The staff's statement of aims presented to the parents was as follows:

1. To encourage all children to live in social harmony.
2. To encourage children to think for themselves and make their own decisions about their learning and their lives.
3. To ensure that each child can read, express himself/herself clearly and thoughtfully in language.
4. To ensure that each child is well-grounded in basic mathematics.
5. To provide a wide choice of activities and interests for a child to experience and enjoy in a stable environment.

In her critique, Walker admits that most of those points are 'common ground', only objecting to the second, and adding a point about preparing children for secondary school. If she had this vast area of agreement with her colleagues, why did she attack them on July 9th? She made no more attempt then to discuss the five points than she did to enlarge on her paper.

More importantly, Walker never admitted on July 9th what she was secretly saying to parents and others, about alleged political motivation of her colleagues. She was not so reticent in her letters to

50

Boyson. In September 1975 she was to write 'Mr Ellis and his staff made no secret of the fact . . . that their aim is to change society.' The staff had said nothing of the kind as far as schools were concerned, but Walker continues: 'the method by which they hope to achieve this is to turn out a generation of semi-literate, anti-authoritarian, anti-establishment, ignorant, frustrated, aimless young people, quick to anger, emotionally immature, who have been spoiled for secure jobs, and having large chips on their shoulders will readily follow the first little gauleiter who shows them how to channel their frustrations into violent action to further revolutionary ends.' Here we are back to Lynn's 'internal enemies'. Walker was, at the time of the inquiry, most anxious that the questioning should uncover the alleged political motives of Ellis and Haddow.

The chronology has shown, and will continue to show, the proliferation of political rumours about Tyndale. The staff were presented as extreme left-wing child indoctrinators, bent on producing the 'human dust' of revolution. They were therefore to find themselves in a permanently defensive position. Walker was by no means politically naive, but was never called upon to justify the political bases of her opinions. Her view could be presented as a defence of the status quo, which did not need to be justified. The other teachers' view could make no such claims, and could be presented as 'politics'. Those with firmly established power always claim to act with strict neutrality, while accusing radical opponents of being political. It was convenient to ignore Walker's radicalism, and use her views to attack, in a purely tactical way, those whom they saw, rightly or wrongly, as more dangerous.

Chapter 5
July–October 1974

This period saw a hardening of attitudes of staff and their critics, a
brief flare-up, followed by the apparent peace of a 'supportive'
managers' resolution. The staff were putting their philosophy into
practice under pressure, though a useful start had been made. In
retrospect it is obvious the events led some to believe the only
satisfactory solution would be the removal of Ellis and his
replacement by Hart.

Much has been made of parental complaints in 1974. It has been
shown that two Infant parents had written letters about the Juniors'
in early July; Ellis had received copies. Unknown to him, however,
three other letters existed from the same period. One, from an
Infant parent who had known Ellis at Charles Lamb, expressed
sympathy with his problem, and suggested support from the
Authority. Two others, from Junior parents, Erwin and Saunders,
were critical. Erwin had disagreed on occasions with Ellis, once quite
strongly about some matters of her child's education, and her
remark about Haddow's class had provoked the staff walk-out on
July 9th. Shortly after this event she wrote her complaint to
Divisional Office and County Hall, a highly-coloured account of her
interviews with Ellis, with strong aspersions about his fitness for

headship.

Saunders had gone to Australia with her child in autumn 1973 and only returned in summer 1974. After five days she removed her child. Her letter, however, gave the impression she was well-acquainted with the school, and totally dissatisfied. She and Erwin were friends of Gittings, who admitted she might have suggested that Saunders write to Divisional Office.

On July 15th, Deputy Divisional Officer Norman Kalber informed TS13, the teachers' disciplinary department of ILEA, about Walker's document. Wales had a telephone conversation with TS13 on July 22nd; on the 24th all five letters from parents were gathered together and sent to TS13. The Erwin letter containing 'more specific complaints about Mr Ellis. was also sent to Chief Inspector Michael Birchenough.

The affair of Walker's 'unprofessional conduct' and the parental complaints became strangely linked at TS13, which sent a letter of advice to Divisional Office on August 6th. This lists three courses of action open to Ellis in the Walker affair. It then expands on the difficulties he might have in substantiating charges against Walker for the production and distribution of her paper. It states that Walker should be advised informally of the unwiseness of her conduct and, having established that she has acted 'unofficially', gives advice on how she can make her complaints official, through the managers. It notes the parental complaints, and suggests the ILEA might investigate them 'by way of a visitation', to alleviate Walker's qualms. One would be forgiven for assuming from this minute that Ellis is the defendant and Walker preferring charges.

TS13 were not in possession of all the facts, or were ignoring some. It was Wales's duty to supply them with full information, so they could make a complete recommendation. Yet no mention is made of Haddow's letter of complaint. And what about the attack Walker made on Ellis at a public meeting, witnessed by Rice? Heads attacked by members of staff are usually backed by the ILEA: but not here.

The possible courses of action in the letter are suspicious. Firstly, Ellis could take up Walker's conduct with the Union. Secondly, he could circulate a document refuting hers. The principle appears to be that if a teacher attacks the head in print, the head replies in kind. What if other teachers join in? Is a pamphlet war being sanctioned? In a democratic organisation this would be acceptable, but no authority regards school as a democracy. It is a hierarchy, the head the untouchable top.

The third course was for Ellis to use ILEA's official complaints procedure. But TS13 themselves thought he would have trouble making the complaint stick. He might have gone ahead—though a disciplinary procedure could have been fatal for the school, since it might have polarized parents. Could he count on the managers' support? At least two, Gittings and Burnett, had been in secret contact with Walker. It was possible the procedure could have been turned against him, and those who supported him and opposed Walker, especially Haddow. Ellis was never told the details of the TS13 minute, so an informed decision was impossible.

Other courses were open, though not listed in the minute. According to the rules of management, the managing body could lay a complaint. Although they had not nominated Ellis, they had been instrumental in appointing him, and it is incumbent on managers to support the head. Many of them had witnessed Walker's attack; most, however, lacked information about the vital events of the period. Ellis and Haddow were to try in vain to put these facts before them.

Finally, ILEA could have found Walker another post. This was the simplest way out; yet it never seems to have occurred to them. Why not?

On August 28th Rice interviewed Walker. He pointed out that her involvement of July 9th had not been helpful. She agreed—and apologised to him! She was, nevertheless, glad that he understood her problems. He in turn 'sympathised' (his words) with her, but told her she must cooperate with the staff. As Ellis put it at the inquiry: 'I was expecting Rice to come down on Walker like a ton of bricks; instead, I learned he'd hit her on the arm with a powder-puff.'

ILEA's reaction to the Walker affair and the complaints is hard to unravel. Wales and Kalber retired in mid-1975, and did not give evidence at the inquiry. No official from TS13 was called. An unsatisfactory, equivocal air pervades the whole business.

The same could be said of what took place on July 23rd: the four managers went to meet Rice, and were confronted with three other officials—Wales, Kalber and Buxton. This meeting is a milestone, as much for what it came to represent as for what was discussed, although that is of considerable interest. It was an example of the secret dealing that characterises the politics of education. Why Ellis was not invited will always be a mystery: so much of the mistrust engendered would have been avoided.

Two versions were to filter back to the staff—one from the officials, another from Fairweather. Neither fitted the note that was taken (which was not revealed until the inquiry), or was calculated to give the teachers confidence for the start of the school year. They felt these secret dealings were being carried on regardless of the problems they were facing in their work, and of the interests of the school.

Ellis received the first version when he was invited to Divisional Office on September 2nd to see Wales and Rice. The only TS13 option revealed to him was making a complaint under the professional conduct procedure of the NUT. This was impossible, because Walker was not a member. Wales told TS13 on September 3rd that Ellis would take no 'professional action'. Ellis was not to be told of all the TS13 options until September 23rd.

Ellis gained the impression the managers were hostile, and were giving him to the end of the year to make good, before they would press for an inquiry. The two officials appeared sympathetic, professing to see in the managers a group anxious for 'overnight' changes in schools.

Ellis left this meeting profoundly depressed. It seemed the pressures of the previous term were to be renewed before the school had even got properly started. The roll had fallen to 156, a worrying fact, but one that had a bright side, since it meant an improved teacher-pupil ratio and a more favourable chance for staff policies. Rice's extra money was coming into the school. The signs were, in a number of ways, promising; but this promise would be destroyed if Tyndale were hit by the same storms as the previous term.

At the inaugural staff meeting of September 4th, the old wounds immediately opened. Ellis and Haddow had been in contact with the NUT about the events of the previous term. Walker's political allegations about Haddow had been placed in the hands of the NUT solicitor, who had written to her on August 2nd. Haddow made the point that no frank discussion of the future was possible until the events of last term had been cleared up, and as long as there was the danger of garbled versions of staff views being exported to parents and others. (During this month Walker drafted a long letter to Rice full of what purported to be staff opinions; in October she wrote again to Boyson.)

Walker became very animated, insisted that managers and parents had wanted her to produce the 'Black Paper', but still refused to give names. The staff felt they had a right to know if managers had been behaving improperly. When it was suggested the school might be under attack, Walker scoffed at the idea, and Ellis felt he had to reveal what he had gathered from the Divisional Office meeting.

Thus, in the very first week, the pressure was on again. Rice advised that Walker be excluded from staff meetings, but acted no further.

The school was now organised on different lines. The oldest children were in separate classes, with Felton and Chowles. To avoid friction, Walker worked exclusively with Chowles. The youngest children were in a co-operative teaching group with McWhirter and McColgan, who were faced simultaneously with an advantage and a drawback. Only 28 children had transferred from the Infants', but most were in the lower ability range, many extremely disturbed, and one third had minimal reading attainment. Yet, only a year later, the Junior School was to be held solely responsible by the inspectors for the low attainment of these pupils.

These two teachers were faced with what was, in many ways, one large remedial group. The rest of the children were organised in a teaching team. This was, structurally, the least conventional aspect of the school, and was attacked consistently in the inquiry. Certain managers had decided that it would not work. Yet Haddow, Green, Austin and Richards had worked in a team before, the organisation had been thoroughly discussed the previous term, and the teachers had spent the last week of the holidays preparing their rooms and work.

In the search for reasons why the team was singled out for attack, one suggests itself immediately—Haddow was its leader. For reasons unconnected with his teaching, he was being seen in the role that Walker had cast for him, the malign influence, the trouble-maker. She saw him as 'dangerous', and considered he over-influenced others, including Ellis.

Haddow's Svengali-like control of Ellis is another persistent Tyndale fiction. A study could be written on how Walker's myths were fleshed out by others, and justified by 'evidence'. The managers pursued an anti-Haddow line in much of their evidence at the

56

inquiry. But then he was teacher-manager, and these are supposed to be docile yes-men, whereas he presented his views forcefully, which tended to upset people. Buxton characterised him as 'a good teacher, but a strong personality'. Note the 'but', and also the 'good teacher': even Walker never denied this. Why did his work always come in for heavy criticism?

The team developed, working on a system of 'closed' sessions when basic skills were pursued, and 'open' sessions where a wide range of options were offered. For the 'open sessions' the hall and corridors were work areas; the 'closed' sessions were confined to classrooms, with Haddow taking out small groups needing special help. Later, he and Austin set up an additional, voluntary remedial reading system within the team.

Early in the term the managers' visits began. Gittings was complaining about broken milk-bottles from the previous term. Burnett came in on September 11th, and was taxed by Ellis with the July 23rd meeting. She did not agree with the officials' version, and refused to name the other managers involved. She had the impression the meeting was confidential. But if the managers, as they later claimed, were seeking ways of improving the school, secrecy would seem to be pointless, even counter-productive, since leaks would lead to the most sinister constructions being put on the gathering.

The strain on the staff in these early weeks was noticeable. Newcomers Austin and Felton sensed the apprehension stemming from the knowledge of the July 23rd meeting. At this point, with the exception of Chowles and Walker, they decided all managers should know about the events of last term, and the way the staff felt about them. They wanted their position made clear from the start, to avoid any repetition of what had happened before. The first staff statement was sent to the managers on September 16th, with copies to Divisional Office and County Hall. It outlined the problems of the school, previous events, and asked for firm support. It was a strong, even aggressive, document. Manager Tennant was amazed, because it bore no resemblance to the situation 'as he saw it'. But what was Tennant seeing? Like most other managers, he had little idea of what had been going on; what he did know could only have been gleaned from managers' meetings, where the real facts were never allowed into the open, or from Labour Party colleagues like Burnett, whose view was necessarily coloured. The staff's point of view had never been put to him, and he was not to visit the school until January 1975.

57

On September 18th, the staff received the second revised
version of the July 23rd meeting from Fairweather, making her first
official visit to the school. She named the other managers at the
meeting, and the other officials. Her version differed substantially
from the previous one, and contained enough to arouse
apprehension and anger among the staff. According to her the
following matters had been put by the officials to the managers: the
removal of the head and re-organisation of the school; an inquiry, to
be set up early in 1975; closure of the school when the roll fell
under 80; press leaks might stir up trouble for the teachers; a
teacher-spy could be appointed to report back on staff activities.

In the official note there are matters which relate to much of
Fairweather's version, though not in the manner in which she put
them. The difficulty of terminating a head's contract was discussed,
as was the viability of the school if the roll fell below 80.
Information was also sought by managers on the ILEA's inquiry
procedures. It is interesting, on these and some of Fairweather's
other points, that some managers were to come to the conclusion
that Ellis should be removed, that press leaks were to be made, that
there was eventually an inquiry. On the matter of a teacher reporting
on staff activities, Walker had in fact done, and was to continue to
do, just this.

The official note shows that McColgan was mentioned, and that
Rice thought her a 'competent teacher'. What it does not show is
Buxton's off-the-record comments. A document submitted to the
inquiry by Dewhurst is most illuminating. She writes, 'During the
meeting . . . Mr. Buxton asked Miss Parks [clerk to the managers]
to stop taking notes, and then confided that Divisional Office were
having to deal with an exceptionally difficult group of people. He
talked of the difficulties of Mrs McColgan over Highbury Quadrant,
and at other schools, and inferred [sic] that this group would, and
indeed had, practised intimidation over anyone who either got in
their way, or would not toe their particular line. As I remember it,
he inferred [sic] that they had tried to get at him, and had made life
particularly difficult and unpleasant for him.'

What was the purpose of this in an educational discussion? If it
were relevant to the running of the school, why was it not included
in the official note? At a meeting ostensibly designed to seek ways
of support, such rumours were not calculated to give managers
confidence in the school, and would simply confirm what was being

circulated in the area by political scare-mongering. In summer 1974, a teacher had reported to the Tyndale staff an alleged remark of Buxton's : 'The solution to Tyndale might be to replace the head by a right-wing, formal bastard.' Taxed with this in the inquiry, Buxton admitted he might have said it, but if he had, it had been a joke.

Fairweather retailed other stories—of local educationalists and teachers willing to give evidence against Tyndale teachers in an inquiry, of a local councillor stating that the head should be removed in order that action could be taken against Haddow and McColgan, of the militant group of North London teachers active in smashing the system. All wild stories, one might say? But again the same themes—inquiry, removal of Ellis, militant teachers.

As a result of Fairweather's visit, a strong demand for support was sent by the staff to Burnett on September 19th. Frankel, one of the parents approached by Walker on July, sent a telegram to ILEA leader Ashley Bramall, deploring the political scare-mongering. She received no reply. Two others, Caryl and David Harter, wrote to Burnett, reiterating their support for the school's policy.

Dewhurst had come to the end of her term as parent-manager, and on September 19th an election for her successor was held. Newman, who had spoken against Walker on July 9th, was proposed. With no other nominations, he should have been declared elected. However, Gittings, though acting as returning officer, suggested to others that they stand against him. He still won.

On the afternoon of September 20th, Mabey arrived unannounced in McColgan's class. He did not introduce himself, but just stood there watching her. He said Ellis had no right to insist on appointments. 'Things' might be going on. What 'things'? He did not specify. According to his inquiry evidence, he had come to see if political indoctrination was being practised. He found none. But while at the school he did repeat other political rumours. The teachers were producing 'cannon fodder' for revolution by boring children; children were playing 'Monopoly' to learn how to smash capitalism. Again, ludicrous stories, unworthy of note in any serious assessment. But are they? Later on, many newspapers had no such qualms, and the red-baiting bandwagon rolled with vengeance. 'Mr Haddow wanted to destroy society, didn't he?' asked barrister John Williams of Ellis, during the inquiry.

At the managers' meeting of September 23rd it was decided to hold a special meeting on October 7th, to consider the curricula and the staff statements. Wales reported to the managers the options open to Ellis in the Walker affair, but did not make it clear they could make their own complaint. Attempts made by Haddow to raise the matter for discussion were prevented, on the grounds that Walker and Dewhurst were not present. Wales was later asked by Haddow if these two could attend the next meeting, but on October 2nd replied that he had been 'advised' this was not in order. ILEA has its own versions of Catch-22.

On September 24th, Conservative ILEA Member Baker came to the school. Ellis did not know she had spoken against his appointment, and did not question her reasons for visiting. He explained the situation, and sought her help. She suggested contacting Hinds, requesting him to receive a staff delegation.

That evening, in the absence of Ellis and Chowles, Rice attended a staff meeting. The staff explained their worries, instancing the number of managerial visits and the disquieting information that had reached them. He refuted the 'Fairweather' version of the July 23rd meeting, promised support, but would not make it public. After this meeting, Walker again claimed managerial support for her actions, and instanced a note of thanks sent to her by Burnett after July 9th.

The letter the staff drafted to Hinds outlined their worries, feared frank discussion would be prevented at the October managers' meeting, and asked him to receive a deputation. Hinds, in his reply of October 4th, indicated he had been assured by officials that no complaint had been received about the staff. This was untrue; such complaints were in the hands of TS13. He also asserted that the managers' meeting would be fair. There was a complaints procedure, he wrote. But he omitted the fact that the managers had not been assured of their own power of complaint, nor could the procedure be used against managers who had behaved improperly. As for the falling roll, this was natural in a declining area. Yet how could a fall from 218 to 156 in a few months be 'natural'? He would not receive a deputation and there is no indication of his taking any action following the staff's letter.

In itself, it may not have rung an alarm bell. But he had been sent a copy of the staff's first statement. Hinds was a busy man, but even a cursory reading of that document must have convinced him of one of two things: either the majority of staff were insane, or there was something in what they said. Whatever the case, some positive action was necessary. One must contrast Hinds' inaction with his response in June 1974 (and later in February 1975), when managerial concern about Tyndale came through the Labour Party network.

During September Walker was busy on a long document, which was finally sent to Rice. Like many Walker documents, it went through various drafts, most of which were available to the inquiry. They all contain attacks on those who do not agree with her. Ellis and Haddow are denigrated, sometimes with pure fantasies. Ellis, according to Walker, does not believe in reading, writing, remedial work, maths or secondary schools. She suggests: 'Perhaps the answer is for Mr Ellis to be promoted sideways or something—he must be good for some job, but it isn't headship.' Haddow is accused of introducing total children's rights, and bringing chaos to the school, of being 'dangerous', and of slandering other teachers. He is even obliquely criticised for staying silent in some meetings, this being Walker's proof that he is, in some sinister way, directing the opinions of others. No other member of staff is given credit for independent thought, McColgan being insultingly described as 'a nonentity'. Since neither Rice nor Walker ever informed the staff of this letter, they had no chance to combat these allegations.

At the managers' meeting of October 7th attempts by Ellis, Haddow and Newman to give the facts behind the staff statements were prevented, by the reiteration that there was a perfectly adequate complaints procedure, and that Walker was not present. Haddow tried to substantiate the claims of political harassment without mentioning Walker, but the managers washed their hands of the business, and affirmed their own innocence by passing a resolution, proposed by Mabey, that 'political harassment' did not refer to them.

When Ellis put forward the Fairweather version of the July 23rd meeting, Wales did not deny it, but called it a 'gross breach of confidence'. Yet he had given his own version on September 2nd. Many managers were concerned they had not been informed of this secret meeting.

There was a lengthy discussion about curricula. Having 'considered' these, the managers passed a resolution of support for the *aims* of both schools. They enshrined this 'supportive' resolution in a letter to parents on October 16th. Here, the word 'considered' had been changed to 'received'. At the inquiry, the managers claimed Ellis had demanded this change from Divisional Office. But officers of the North London Teachers Association had visited the school, and had been told the facts to date. They were concerned that managerial support should not seem dependent on approval of the curriculum, since this was the thin end of the wedge. It could open all sorts of unpleasant doors, leading to a situation where managers might test their powers very effectively over teachers. NLTA pressure brought about the change in wording.

Tennant later described the resolution of October 7th as 'papering over the cracks'. On the surface it seemed that at last the managers publicly supported the staff. Tyndale settled to a period of calm, productive development—until a new set of events became known in April 1975. The conflict had not ended, but simply gone underground. Now more powerful forces were at work.

Chapter 6
Parents and Children

The word 'accountability' has crept into use more and more in recent years. It is an ill-defined term, used by progressives advocating more involvement of local communities in schools, and by traditionalists seeing the possibilities for its use, particularly with parents, as a tactic to put pressure on progressive schools. Its meaning is unclear, though it centres round the idea that persons involved in providing education should in some way be responsible to groups who have particular interests in a school. Who these groups should be, and the degree to which educationalists should be responsible to them, is not easy to decide.

Under the 1944 Education Act LEAs have a duty to provide education suitable to the requirements of children in their areas. ILEA delegates the running of the schools to managers and heads, but gives no clear indications what a suitable education might be, leaving this to heads and managers. Nor does it give any precise definition as to where the teachers' responsibility ends and the managers' begins, or how far each group involved, including the authority itself, is responsible to the other groups for the interpretation and administration of its duties.

The extent to which each group can be held accountable to parents is also unclear, as parents have few defined 'rights' though they do have 'duties'. The 1944 Act states: 'It shall be the duty of every parent of every child of compulsory school age to cause him to receive efficient full-time education suitable to his age, ability and aptitude, either by regular attendance at school or otherwise.' If parents are negligent in this they face prosecution.

Their rights to choose a type of education they consider 'efficient' and 'suitable' for their child are not so definite. Section 76 of the Act reads: 'the Ministry and Local Education Authority shall have regard to the principle that, so far as it is compatible with the provision of efficient instruction and training and the avoidance of unreasonable expenditure, pupils are to be educated in accordance with the wishes of the parent.' Parents have a legal duty to ensure their child receives adequate education, while the Authority need only have regard to the principle of parental choice.

The rights which parents have are extremely limited. The rights which ILEA grants to parents are equally limited. No directive is given to heads that parental opinion should be considered in the formulation of school policy. No clear indication is given of how much information parents should be provided with, or how far a school's policies should be acceptable to them. The constitution of the managing body allows for only one parent representative: parental influence is minimal.

There is also no procedure for dealing with parents' complaints. Those sent in by Tyndale parents were not investigated, but stored up until the inquiry, five of them for over a year. Although it was obvious from the falling roll that children were being removed, the Authority refused to investigate this show of 'parental discontent', until the issue had reached the press, and they could no longer ignore it.

All this leaves parental involvement open to manipulation, not only by the Authority, but by other groups. The interpretation of the degree to which teachers should be controlled by parental opinion, and the encouragement given to parents to fight for this control, can be tempered to specific situations.

It can be seen how Walker tried to use parents to put pressure on staff to adopt 'traditional' teaching methods, thus suggesting parents should have a right to decide school policies. But if teachers are to be bound by parents' decisions, problems arise. Parents are

64

not a group with similar aspirations for their children. It is not possible to satisfy all the groups within an Inner London school: the satisfaction of one often means the alienation of another. This was particularly true at Tyndale, which had an original intake from vastly differing social backgrounds. If the teachers had acceded to pressures from the parents Walker had rallied, and had changed their policies accordingly, the resulting formal methods would certainly not have satisfied the 'progressive' parents.

If teachers opt for satisfying the majority group, there can still be problems. Not only is it possible to have a large minority who are out of sympathy with the school, but minority groups, particularly of the articulate middle-class type, can bring more pressure to bear than a larger, less articulate group. This can lead to the domination of meetings and committees by a minority.

What happens if staff, and even the local inspectorate who advise them on behalf of the Authority, are out of sympathy with parents' views? Should they change carefully chosen policies, which they consider to be in the best interests of the children, to fit in with parents' wishes?

At Tyndale, it can be seen how the actions of individuals might have led parents to remove their children from the school. The resulting fall in roll was used as proof that there was something wrong. But because a school is 'unpopular', it does not mean it is bad. It is possible for a good informal school, in an area where most parents opt for 'traditional' methods, to be at risk, as well as a school whose reputation has suffered from the most unjust criticisms. In a period of economic recession and falling birthrate, schools are forced to compete with each other for survival, and impressive displays of work which bear no relation to the realities become even more prevalent, as schools court parents. Head teachers become even more obsessed with public relations and, as some schools succeed, a form of selection in primary education appears, in which schools that are full can choose their pupils. A much more competitive education system results.

Perhaps the interpretation of 'accountability' most readily accepted is that teachers should provide parents with as much information as possible about their policies and methods, and should try to involve them in the school in an attempt to gain their support. This concept was developed in the late 1960s. Until that time schools had been the privileged domain of the head teachers and their staff; most still are. Parents were kept at a distance by stringent appointment systems. They were kept in the dark as to the true nature of the school, their only information being provided at specially staged open evenings, when the 'best' work was on display, which revealed exactly what the school wanted to reveal, and no more. Teachers and heads relied on their 'professional mystique' to fend off adverse criticisms, and to keep decisions concerning methods and policies within their grasp. When parents did visit they were blinded as much by the 'teacher's science' as by the lack of information. Problems were usually glossed over—to admit a school had them was to admit an inability to cope; the system does not allow for such admissions.

The situation has improved considerably in some schools. More meetings are held to discuss methods as well as children's work. Parents are encouraged to help, either directly within the classroom, or by collecting money through organising sales and fairs. In many schools parent-teacher associations have been set up, to organise and co-ordinate staff/parent efforts. The Plowden report cites instances of swimming pools and other expensive equipment being financed through the efforts of such associations.

Yet Plowden found that a smaller proportion of manual workers attended PTA meetings than any other school function. It seems this is not the most effective way of involving this group in school activities. Plowden, while supporting the existence of such groups, says: 'we do not think that PTAs are necessarily the best means of fostering close relationships between home and school. They can be of the greatest value where good leadership is given by the head. They may do harm if they get into the hands of a small group.' At Tyndale, Ellis' relationships with parents were soured by the intervention of others who had been involved with the school for some years, before he had been there long enough to establish his position with parents. Although not against PTAs in principle, the teachers recognised that if one had been set up at Tyndale during the period of attack it might have done considerable harm, as it could easily have got into the hands of a small group, who might have used it to further their own interests.

The teachers therefore chose other methods of involving parents. They went to considerable lengths to ensure the success of this project. Parents were encouraged to visit at any time, with or without appointments, to discuss their children with the teacher, or

66

to assist in the school's work. A coffee area was set up for their use. Parents of children with difficulties were asked to co-operate in trying to cope with their problems. Numerous open evenings and meetings were held, to discuss policies and developments. Response to such meetings had always been poor, so staff visited parents to encourage attendance. Haddow sent a questionnaire to parents of children in his class, asking for comments on an option system he had introduced.

Any ILEA school has problems. The teachers did not try to hide this fact from parents, and did not make empty promises about possible achievements, but tried to present the situation as it was. Parents were provided with more information than ever before. Some did support the efforts of the school: they accompanied children and teachers on visits, and organised money-raising activities. One parent came in each week to take a group for cookery, another organised a drama project. Dull brown noticeboards were brightly painted with the assistance of other parents, and one child who showed problems was helped considerably by his mother coming to the school each afternoon to work with him. Others also helped in the classroom.

Parents and teachers became more friendly, and as the 'mystique' of teaching began to disappear the teachers became more vulnerable, as parents felt more able to approach and even criticise them. No school can satisfy all its parents, and the more information parents have about it, the easier it is to find fault. It is also easy to use those 'faults' as evidence of below-standard teaching, in order to manipulate arguments in essence ideological. This was to happen at Tyndale.

Schools present one of the few 'competitive industries' where the customer and consumer belong to different groups. It is assumed the parent knows what is best for the child, being the adult most closely involved in and responsible for the child's upbringing. The parent has ownership of that child, except in circumstances where the situation goes drastically wrong.

But do parents know what is best for their children? How often do they try to compensate for their inadequacies and failures through their children's academic achievements? How often do parents see their children as extensions of themselves, in some way reflecting their capabilities. How often do they force their own aspirations upon them, even if in doing so they distress the children?

The teacher is often the first 'outside' adult children come into contact with who has some responsibility for their upbringing. What should teachers do if what they believe to be best for the development of a child is at variance with the beliefs of the parent? Because it is parents who have more control over choice of school, it is usually parents whom the teacher tries to satisfy, rather than the child. At Tyndale some parents believed it was 'best' for their children to be hit, so that they would learn to obey. Not only did most of the staff disagree with this theory, it is against ILEA's rules to hit primary children. Teachers, even within their terms of employment, cannot always satisfy parents' wishes, and the Authority itself is at variance with some parents on this issue.

Few people talk about parents' and teachers' accountability to children. Within the 1944 Act children are given no positive rights; and even within the ILEA's rules, although they have a right not to be hit, they still have no positive rights. Having no say at all in the choice of education, or in the way it is administered, the child becomes the receiver of whatever the relevant body decides to dish out. Few parents or teachers consult children about their education.

At Tyndale the teachers decided the children should be given as much choice and responsibility as the limitations of a school will allow. They were encouraged to consider the school as their building, could come in before school, stay afterwards, and have the choice of going out or staying in at playtimes. Common teacher/children areas were set up for use at these times. The segregation of playgrounds, introduced by Chowles and Hart, was discontinued, along with the separation of boys' and girls' activities. Football was no longer the territory of boys, needlework no longer confined to girls. Rules were reduced to a minimum, and children were expected to exercise a responsibility commensurate with the rights given to them. A wide range of activities, both academic and non-academic, were offered within an option system.

Such a democratic system produces problems. Many children have been conditioned by their parents and their previous experiences to expect a certain type of school. In his statement to the inquiry Haddow described the reactions of children in his class to the introduction of an option system. He found the children who seemed to derive most benefit were at two extremes, the most academically able, usually from middle-class homes, and those children who normally have difficulty in adjusting to school, 68 including the most socially and emotionally deprived.

The 'brighter' children were often from more 'liberal' homes, where they were allowed more independence and freedom. Their parents might have a more realistic attitude to teachers, being less susceptible to their professional mystique. With the freer system, these children were able to pursue in great depth activities that interested them. One child, from an extremely 'liberal' intellectual background, would react to suppression by refusing to work, but thrived within the option system, being able to pursue his scientific interests. His projects were often complex, involving such calculations as the cubic capacity of a ton of water.

The other successful group, the children with difficulties, are the failures of many schools. Because of their problems they often cannot compete academically. In most systems they are alienated more and more as they are constantly faced with their own failures; they either become aggressive or withdraw. Within the freer system this group initially reacted in a similar way to the middle group. They are conditioned to see a teacher as someone who tells them what to do, an authority figure who should make them obey, rather like a policeman. There is an inherent hostility towards such figures. These children are confused by teachers who do not fit the image, and at first react against them: it takes time to gain their confidence.

After the initial problems, this group made great progress at Tyndale. They were able to choose activities of more relevance to them, and gain in confidence through success in particular areas. The choice provided was wide, with activities which included, swimming, ice-skating, drama, games, French, creative writing, art and craft, woodwork, cookery, special visits and science. Children who had previously been very nervous benefited. One girl, a diabetic, who was not only very delicate and shy, but also missed school for long periods through illness, became more outward going and confident, and made considerable advances in her reading within the team.

It was the middle group who responded least favourably. They often came from the more aspiring working-class homes, were so well conditioned to obey adults, and unused to thinking for themselves, that they had difficulties in adjusting. They too saw the teacher as an authority figure and, with constant reinforcement from parents, saw more 'liberal' attitudes as weakness. This was the group that had most frequently to be directed to options, and needed continual assistance with them, as they were unable to take initiatives. They also tended to opt for the less demanding, more mechanical tasks. They saw school as a place to work, and had a very narrow concept of what work was. Anything that seemed like play was a waste of time.

For them the quality of education lay in the amount of 'work' they did, and academic success was based on quantifiable levels of achievement. They required comparisons by which to measure their achievements. One child in this group not only wanted to do a project on butterflies herself, but wanted her teacher to compel the rest to work on the same project, in order to prove her work was of a higher standard. The methods employed at Tyndale did not encourage such competition. The staff saw this as a stage of development which these children would have to go through in order to become self-motivated. By the end of the school year they were adjusting to this approach.

It was this group which received most negative reinforcement of the school's methods at home. Parental attitudes not only influence a child's attitudes to school, but also affect achievement. Some parents made false distinctions between work and play, with work being 'interesting' and 'valuable' and play a waste of time. Children were led to believe they were doing nothing worthwhile and that they were bored. This is the normal reaction of parents to 'progressive' schools. It was to these parents that Walker's arguments and criticisms were most attractive. It was also this conditioning, combined with the more obvious hostility against the teachers at the time of the strike in September 1975, that led to many of the statements to the press concerning alleged playing of board games all day at Tyndale.

There are many sub-divisions of reaction within these groupings of children. One of the most interesting is the difference of attitude of boys and girls. Through their conditioning girls are generally more amenable to school, and create fewer problems for the teacher: this was true at Tyndale. Although all activities were open to boys and girls, boys still tended to keep away from needlework and girls from football. The few children who did participate in both types of activities were usually from the most emotionally deprived group.

The attitudes towards school that parents were expressing and passing on to their children were not conditioned solely by the methods employed, but also by rumours and gossip. The attack on the school had not only come from Walker's group of followers, but

70

also from some of the middle class who, while wanting the same results as the aspiring working class, wanted them to be obtained through more 'liberal' methods.

Instead of opting for putting all their efforts into satisfying this group, which could wield the most power, perhaps at the expense of other children, the Tyndale staff concentrated on the disadvantaged child, and in accordance with their policies of greater involvement of parents were completely open about this. This led to pressure, both from the aspiring working class, who already felt hostility towards this group of families, and the middle clas, who wanted the school run exclusively for their children. The hostilities that had been built up came to a head at the meeting of June 13th 1974 which, ironically, had been called in order to explain the staff's actions over the London Allowance campaign, and involve parents even more in their actions.

Why did this initially small group of hostile parents increase? Why did some parents who had been supportive until September 1975 suddenly change their minds? Obviously once an attack on a school has been staged many parents, even among those not totally taken in by the stories, are alerted, and believing there is no smoke without fire, are looking for evidence to 'prove' the case. Many of those parents who had been made suspicious by the attacks of summer 1974 were never really to support Tyndale.

A huge majority of parents who were to attack the school so violently during the strike of September 1975 had recent connections with the Infant School. The children of parents who were most willing to damn the striking teachers to the press and at the inquiry were in the first two years of the Junior School, all transferred from the Infants' since September 1974. This group often had no direct knowledge of the school before their children had transferred, and the transfer had occured after the attack had started. In her evidence to the inquiry Margaret Ford, former Infant teacher, stated that enquiries made to Infant staff concerning the Junior School were met with a 'studied silence'. The only information these parents were receiving about the Juniors' were tales of political subversion and educational incompetence: nothing was being done to inspire confidence.

This was to have an effect on the children. Those children that transferred in 1974 proved to be extremely difficult. Had they been led to believe that they were attending a 'bad' school, and were acting accordingly? It took a good part of the year for the teachers to gain their confidence. Some of their parents, through their direct knowledge of the school, did in fact come to support it, and signed a petition of support as late as July 1975. But when the school was again publicly attacked in September they were willing to believe anything, including the fact that although their children had been able to read on leaving the Infants', after three weeks in the Juniors' they were unable to. Even the inspectors were to support the theory that the striking teachers had caused the instantaneous wreck of these children, blaming the Junior School for their 'deep-seated problems'.

The school is the nearest institution for the parent to scapegoat when problems arise with children at home. Parents at Tyndale were willing to believe, with the assistance of Walker, that if the school had been fulfilling its duties of 'civilising' their children, their behaviour at home would improve. The fact that children were difficult at home was used as 'evidence' that the school was deficient. Walker's appraisal of children's difficulties at school does not allow for 'bad parents', only 'bad teachers'.

Some parents are influenced in their attitudes to a school by current fashion. An attack on a school can snowball, as parents are conditioned by local 'trends' and gossip. The education of children is a highly charged subject; suggestions that it is deficient produce hysterical responses. These are heightened at the suggestion of political indoctrination. Both these accusations were to be publicly levelled at the Tyndale staff. The frenzied responses they produced are illustrated by the vicious attacks made by parents to the press. Hinds commented at the inquiry: 'Rumours can destroy a school's reputation overnight. It can take five years to build it up again.'

After all the rumours and attacks the teachers had been subjected to, the parents of 28 children, some of whom would not normally have dreamt of defying authority, were willing to ignore instructions from the ILEA to send their children to Tyndale during the strike. They preferred to send them to Gaskin Street, the school the teachers set up in a local church hall during the strike. These parents, whose children were from the 'brighter' group and that with most difficulties, were satisfied with the education their children received at Tyndale. They not only wanted to show their support for the teachers, but wanted their children to continue being taught by them.

72

Some of this group were more concerned with their children's well-being than with academic aspirations. One parent was to write in his statement to the inquiry that his children liked Tyndale because Ellis cared for them. A child at Gaskin Street said her mother wanted her to stay with her teachers as she knew she would be well looked after. These parents felt the staff were concerned with their children's welfare, and had enough confidence in them not to be influenced by rumours. Many of these parents also supported the staff at the inquiry; their evidence was to show they had based their support on a greater knowledge of the school than of most of the parents who attacked Ellis.

What was ILEA's attitude to those parents who supported the teachers? Which parents were they willing to be 'held accountable to'? The receipt of a telegram of the nature of Frankel's to Bramall, complaining that a political campaign was being organised to dismiss the head of her child's school, must surely have been an extraordinary occurrence at County Hall; yet it provoked no action. The authority did not produce it at the inquiry, nor the letter of support which the Harters had sent to the managers, a copy of which had gone to Divisional Office. They did produce letters of complaint from parents which they had stored up from the previous year. When parents refused to send their children to Tyndale when the permanent staff were absent during the 1975 strike, they received letters from the authority advising them to send their children back. When hostile parents did the same thing on the return of Ellis, Roy Price, the new Divisional Officer, commented to the press: 'There are about six schools in the area where children could be accommodated. It would be possible for them to start on Monday if transfers go through without any hitches. It is the most satisfactory solution, but we want to upset the children as little as possible.' When a supportive parent wished to transfer her child to another school, during the absence of the permanent staff during the inquiry, she was not to be met with such assistance. Finally, when two parents, one of whom regularly helped at the school, came in during the 1975 inspection and were having a break for coffee , Pape told them that they should 'either go and bind books, or leave'.

What is the authority's position on the weight parental opinion should carry in the formulation of school policies? In the Risinghill episode parents, who mainly supported the school, were ignored, and the school was closed. Compton, another Islington primary school, is also to be closed in face of parental opposition. In the Tyndale affair, parental opposition was used both by the authority and other groups to add fuel to their attacks on the teachers. The dispute has illustrated how easily parents can be manipulated to join an attack on a school, and how easily the false concern thus engendered can be used as proof that there is something basically wrong with that school and its teachers.

Chapter 7
October 1974–March

On October 12th Walker wrote to Boyson, congratulating him upon his re-election to Parliament, and regretting he was still in opposition. She included a progress report on Tyndale. 'The school managers are now thoroughly alerted and are, I understand, being very vigilant, and the Divisional Inspector, Mr. D. Rice, is closely involved in trying to bring about an improvement. How successful he will be considering the personnel he has to deal with remains to be seen. My personal view is that given enough rope they will hang themselves, but my own position is a somewhat delicate one in view of the leading part I played in the "parents' revolt" last term.'

She resolved the delicacy of her position in December by leaving to take up a post in a private school. Her replacement was Christine Buckton, a teacher who had her own children in the school and was in sympathy with its philosophy. She worked with both older classes.

Tyndale had not heard the last of Walker: she remained in contact with parents. The inquiry documents contain a letter dated January 15th 1975, which a parent sent to her. It mentions a discussion with Walker about her child's education. Walker had advised that the child, who was in the team, be put in Chowles' class.

Shortly afterwards the child was removed from the school, although his attainment was more than adequate.

Following the managers' 'supportive' letter, the staff sent out a further statement to the managers and the ILEA on November 6th, summarizing their views and making one last effort to get the campaign against them discussed. They suggested a basis for 'a return to a healthy state of respect and co-operation'. They also noted that Gittings, in contradiction of the resolution of support, had withdrawn her child.

The autumn term saw a determined effort to counter the attack. Three open evenings were held by the teaching team, one by the younger classes, and four were set aside for parents of children leaving the following summer. The attendances were not encouraging, a typical experience in Islington. Many of the parents so vociferous about alleged low standards before and after this time never bothered to come and talk to their children's teachers. Parental support takes time to build, and Tyndale was not given much. General meetings were avoided, since nobody was anxious to repeat the experiences of the previous term, and one-to-one discussion seemed more valuable. A number of parents previously critical of the school were won over in this way.

The most original departure was the provision of music therapy for 'difficult' children. Ellis and Austin met ILEA officials, psychologists and welfare officers in November, and put the case for drum therapy. This was approved. One psychologist remarked that this was the first time he had seen such an approach adopted. Austin was already in contact with a local West Indian centre, where some children went for tuition. This attempt to reach 'difficult' children and give them confidence in themselves later blossomed into the William Tyndale Steel Band.

Katharine Arnold, a trainee psychotherapist, joined the staff part-time in late 1975. By January 1977 she had numerous groups organised in the 'sanctuary'. She worked with all kinds of behavioural and emotional problems, from extreme reticence to overt aggression.

At a joint staff meeting on November 26th there was a flood of complaints from the Infant staff about particular Junior children. Ellis promised to deal with any problem, provided it was brought to him at the time.

However, on December 5th Hart approached Wales. It is perhaps 76 understandable that one head, in disagreement with another, should consult the Divisional Officer, but not in order to paint a horrifying picture of slackness, lack of control and violence in the Juniors. She commented adversely on its stock and equipment. More seriously, she cast grave doubts on Ellis's competence, by declaring him incapable of controlling the situation. Most serious of all, she alleged the Junior staff favoured black children, and showed them 'excessive affection', a kind of reverse racism — an amazing allegation from somebody who considered herself a 'progressive'. This charge had been directed at Ellis by an Infant parent only the previous day.

This occurred despite the fact that NUT rules say that it is unprofessional 'for any teacher to make a report on the work or conduct of another teacher without at the time acquainting the teacher concerned with the nature of it.' After she left Wales wrote her complaints down, and these notes, produced as evidence at the inquiry, were the first that staff knew of the meeting and the allegations.

All three Infant ancillary helpers with children in the Juniors' withdrew them this term. The circumstances surrounding one of these, Edwards, need comment. In December she announced the removal of both her children from Junior and Infant schools, because she wanted 'formal' education, which she said neither was providing. She attempted to criticize Hart's competence to Ellis, and to attribute the blame for the Juniors' problem on poor Infant education. In January, however, she wrote a letter to County Hall, attacking Ellis and praising Hart.

Another parent who withdrew her child, Rhoda Kerr, also wrote directly to County Hall, although parents usually contact Divisional Office with complaints. All five letters of complaint in July 1974 had gone there, to be followed shortly by the managerial delegation. Six weeks after the two new complaints had gone to the highest level, some of the same managers took their concern there as well. Like the five other complainants, these two did not give evidence at the inquiry.

Councillor Page now comes back on the scene. She had been in contact with local officials about Tyndale in September. In December-January she proposed to Rice that the Juniors' should be inspected. He passed her suggestion to County Hall, where it did not find favour. Page had never visited, nor did she ever visit, Tyndale.

The crucial event of this period was the appointment of

Elizabeth Hoodless to the managing body. She was eminently equipped for the task she now undertook—the final solution of Tyndale's problems, as envisaged by some managers. Her experience as chairwoman of governors in a large secondary school, the fact that her husband was deputy leader of Islington Borough Council, and she head of a local organisation, Community Service Volunteers—all gave her extensive and powerful contacts in the local council, among managers, in the Labour Party and in ILEA.

This was a big fish to deposit in a small pond like Tyndale. No sooner was she on the managing body than she was taking the lead in the secret dealings of early 1975, which laid the ground for the final stages of the conflict. She had discussed Tyndale before her appointment, and appears to have decided something had to be done. But the school was now settled and functioning well, with a united staff and a definite policy: it only required support. Again it was to get the opposite. Another manager appointed at this time was Adam Roberts, a university lecturer, an old acquaintance of Gittings, and a Labour Party member. With disarming candour, he told the inquiry he had wanted to be appointed to a managing body where there might be 'trouble'. He was soon to get his wishes fulfilled.

At the managers' meeting of January 27th, Ellis and Haddow put a motion that managers should make written reports on visits to the school, in order to make it clear what they had said at any given time. This was rejected. Hoodless said some managers might not be capable of making written reports. One of the most disturbing features of the inquiry was testimony by hindsight, where managers raised damaging criticisms of the school they had not brought up at the time in meetings. Although from June 1974 onwards there was an inquisitorial air about managers' meetings, almost no specific criticisms were uttered about the Juniors'.

On February 11th, Hoodless's secretary contacted the school; Hoodless wished to visit. Ellis was heavily involved with secondary transfer at the time, but offered ample opportunity for a future visit. No further communication was made by Hoodless.

The next day she was discussing Ellis with Rice. (She told the inquiry she was worried about Ellis' health.) She was soon in touch with yet another Islington inspector, Roy Truman. She was concerned about the school, she said; she and other managers would like Hart as head of a re-organised Tyndale. Ellis was to be eased gently sideways (as Walker had advocated in her letter to Rice). It

78

never became clear which managers wanted this in early 1975, but one could offer educated guesses. And when had these conclusions been reached? They had certainly not just hit Hoodless like a thunderbolt on February 14th. One fact is clear: only a year after they had been instrumental in his appointment, some people had their knives out for Ellis.

Truman suggested managers express their worries to the political masters at County Hall. But Hoodless had already been working on this line. In late January, she had suggested to Fairweather that a meeting should be sought with Hinds. Fairweather had tried, and failed.

On February 24th Burnett, for domestic reasons, resigned as Chairwoman. She was replaced by Tennant, the shrewd and circumspect secretary of the St. Peter's Ward Labour branch, to which Page and Burnett also belonged. He was yet another 'new Islingtonian', an energetic young professional who moved into the borough in the 1960s. Hoodless immediately complained secretly to him and to Divisional Office that Ellis had rejected her offer of a visit to the school.

But she had now taken the initiative and secured, through her husband, using the Labour Party network, the meeting with Hinds— for February 27th. According to her, Hinds wished the delegation to be 'Labour Party representatives', though he denied this at the inquiry. Infant parent-manager Christina Miles, in evidence to the inquiry, recalled Hoodless saying that they were 'Labour Party representatives' and should not go dressed like 'middle-class trendies' — a fact which caused her to drop out of the delegation.

The other members beside Hoodless were now Fairweather, Gittings and Dewhurst, none of whom were Labour Party members, but all of whom had children in the Infants'. Dewhurst had not even been a manager since July 1974. If parental representatives were needed there was a perfectly capable parent-manager in Newman. But he supported the staff, which seems to have disqualified him from the delegation. Other managers were not informed of the meeting.

The managers took with them criticisms of the Juniors', drawn up by Hoodless from things she had heard other people say, and based on allegations supplied by Gittings and Fairweather, who, together with Tennant, had made a visit to the school on January 17th. At the inquiry it was implied by the managers that Ellis had resented this visit on the grounds that it was to gather evidence against him. This was precisely what it was now being used for.

In July 1975 these notes formed the basis of a press leak by the managers, and thus conditioned from the start the newspapers', and thereby the general public's, view of Tyndale.

It was alleged, for example, that McColgan did not know what maths equipment to order. Yet she had to that date spent hundreds of pounds on such equipment, and this could have been verified by consulting the school files. It was stated that more children from Tyndale were in the remedial classes of a local comprehensive than from any other school. At the inquiry factual evidence, backed by the testimony of teachers in two local secondary schools, showed that Tyndale children were no different in attainment from others. But, as on so many occasions, the staff were given no opportunity to disprove these allegations, since they were never told of them. If the managers had evidence of inefficiency, why did they not carry out their duty to the parents and children, call a meeting, and make a formal complaint? Why this backstairs diplomacy?

There are conflicting versions of the actual meeting. The managers' view was that they were trying to put their concern to the authority, in the hope some improvement could be brought about. They made no recommendations for action, since that was ILEA's business. But they had mentioned, in their 'notes', the possibility of re-organisation.

ILEA explored the re-organisation question thoroughly in March and April, and came up with conclusions. Re-organisation was never undertaken when two heads were still in post, and neither Ellis nor Hart were due to retire until the year 2000. If re-organisation were undertaken, one head would be moved sideways. There was no reason why the Infant head should automatically be appointed: Ellis had experience of a Junior-Infant school, and Hart did not. Nevertheless, for Hoodless, with her desire to remove Ellis, re-organisation must have seemed a solution. Yet re-organisation would not help to bring about the kind of school these managers wanted, unless Hart was its head.

This suggestion was a direct threat to Ellis's position, and although none of the participants said openly at this meeting they wanted him removed, Hinds, with his experience in politics and the Church of England, must have been astute enough to divine what was behind this managerial step. But if he did guess what was in the wind, there was still another problem. Head teachers are difficult to get rid of, except for the most obvious misconduct or inefficiency. Hinds promised the managers he would look into matters, and a further meeting was arranged.

On the ILEA note of the meeting Hinds had written McColgan's name. The managers later alleged he had referred to her as a 'packet of trouble', and implied that they had been less than clever in appointing her. Hinds strongly denied this. Also written was a comment about Ellis's health, implying he had nightmares about the school—a piece of misinformation supplied by Rice. Both ILEA and the clique of managers were showing great interest in Ellis's mental well-being at this point. A collapse on his part would have been a neat solution to all their problems. The managers were to present very strongly the image of a sick, paranoid head in their evidence to the inquiry.

Hinds, in contrast to his response to the teachers' appeal in September 1974, acted promptly, and Rice was asked to make another report. He visited the school on March 4th, and sent in his report on the 11th. He was complimentary about reading standards. Ellis had carefully monitored these, and showed him the results of the tests. Rice wrote, for example; 'In the 3rd year, all but 4 had made progress commensurate with their chronological age.' Reading standards in ILEA schools are not high. Many children leave primary school with a reading age well below their chronological age. The Tyndale achievement was therefore considerable. The reading age figures were fiercely assaulted by the staff's critics at the inquiry. If you are contending that standards are deteriorating, it is inconvenient to be faced with figures which prove they are not. None of the critics could produce contrary figures.

Rice praised some areas, and mentioned others in which he felt less had been achieved. The staff would have agreed they did not have a perfect school. It was a developing one, and all developments are uneven. About the team-teaching Rice said: 'there has been too little structure involved in the curriculum, and the children have been left to their own devices.' But he had not actually seen the team at work; he had never discussed it with Haddow; nor had he spoken to the other teachers. He had no first-hand knowledge on which to base his assessment.

Rice went on: 'Some lack of organisation and educational objectives have caused behavioural problems, which in turn have caused adverse criticism of the school.' How Walker would have approved of that—especially since a large number of the criticisms that Rice knew about had come from interviews with her, and from letters she had written.

Rice is typical of the 'liberal' educationist who will not admit there is a crisis in society, reflected to an extreme degree in inner-urban areas, and that schools, which house the young victims of this crisis, simply reflect what is going on. Tyndale had a clear philosophy at this time, but Rice never inquired what it was. So how did he know its objectives? There was again no intimation of the outside interference that had so plagued the school. What did Rice do? He took the usual way out, and blamed the teachers. 'The headmaster has tried to initiate new patterns of learning without the understanding or cooperation of the parents.' This is Walker's thesis, and ignores all the efforts the staff had been undertaking to contact parents and make them understand.

Meanwhile, rumours about the County Hall meeting were leaking out (though not as far as the teachers). Hinds and Hoodless wrote to each other deprecating this. Confidentiality is the life-blood of closed government.

There is no evidence that any action on the part of ILEA followed the Rice report. Music Inspector Preston visited the school in July, but this was a result of the efforts of Ellis and Austin in connection with the music therapy. They had been trying to contact the Music Inspectorate since December 1974.

On March 26th, Hoodless's private delegation returned to County Hall—minus Dewhurst, but with the addition of Page—at Hinds' invitation. Tennant was not informed of this meeting, nor were the other managers.

Hinds must have seen many assessments of schools. He took the view that Tyndale was no different from any other; no better, no worse. He read extracts from the report, though it is not clear which. But what he read apparently alarmed the delegation, though at the inquiry they could not remember precise details. How far, in fact, were they competent to take an over-all view of London schools, in order to judge Tyndale?

What happened next is a matter of dispute. Hinds maintained he could not act without evidence of the public concern so often cited by the delegation. He needed 'resolutions on his desk'. By this he said he meant the managing body should convene and pass a motion

82

expressing concern. The three managers agreed to do this. But in the inquiry, Page maintained Hinds had encouraged the managers to generate concern, and Hoodless insisted that he was in favour of 'petitions'.

Hinds' view of the meeting was that he was trying to maintain sensible calm, while being assaulted by the vehemence of his questioners. Asked in the inquiry whether Page was 'a hawk or a dove', he replied with feeling 'She was one of a whole flock of hawks.' He complained he was being encouraged to 'use hobnail boots' in an area where he should have been wearing 'ballet shoes'.

Whatever version one accepts, certain questions remain. If Hinds found the school satisfactory, why did he not advise the managers to stop agitating and support it, while himself ensuring his professional advisers also supported it as a matter of urgency? Why was the idea of public concern or a managers' resolution even suggested? If Hinds did not find the school acceptable, why was not a full inspection initiated?

The 'four angry ladies' went away into the ILEA members' bar to discuss the next move. They were now talking of a 'petition'. But if Hinds wanted evidence of concern, the easiest and most open way was full discussion at a properly constituted managers' meeting, followed by a resolution. This group could have convened such a meeting in early April when the Summer Term began, allowing ILEA ample time to act on their resolution. Hoodless made great play in the inquiry of her concern for 'those poor children'. If matters were as urgent as this, why was not the simple course taken? Why did they not ask for an inspection by ILEA? Page, at least, was consistent enough to do so.

But open discussion, from their point of view, would have had tactical drawbacks. It would have revealed the County Hall transactions, not only to the managers, but to the staff. There was the possibility of a split in the managing body, and a strong reaction from the teachers. Inquiry Chairman Auld questioned Hoodless at length on this matter, but even his persistence did not elicit a satisfactory answer. Perhaps their aim was not inspection but re-organisation, in pursuit of Ellis's removal? If so, it would have been counter-productive to try to prove him inefficient, and fail. Hinds' suggestion that the school was, on balance, acceptable meant that it had a good chance of being proved efficient.

83   A more circuitous route was pursued. Hoodless went that

evening to a meeting of the St Mary's Ward branch, where she reported the County Hall transactions, and produced figures which indicated, quite incorrectly, that the roll was still falling. She then moved the following resolution, which was passed:

> 'This St Mary's Ward Branch notes the loss of confidence in the quality of education provided in William Tyndale Junior School, demonstrated by the drop in roll from 249 to 150, and calls on ILEA to investigate urgent action:
>
> a   to provide a proper education to those pupils who remain at the school, and
>
> b   to investigate re-organisation as a J.M. and I. School.'

This resolution was passed to the General Management Committee of the South Islington and Finsbury Labour Party.

After the meeting Hoodless and Alan Pedrick, who with Donald Hoodless and Mabey made up the triumvirate of St Mary's Ward Councillors, discussed and agreed to circulate a petition about the Juniors'. It was, from the start, as the teachers always claimed, a Labour Party, not a public, petition.

While all this energy was being expended, Tyndale marched on purposefully, ruffled briefly by small happenings. On January 23rd the staff, with the exception of Ellis and Chowles, went on strike over the Houghton pay awards. The strikers later received a letter from Briault, stating they were in 'breach of their responsibilities' for absenting themselves to attend demonstrations. They were warned as to their future conduct. They were not told directly that future transgressions would be referred to the managing body for investigation: this information was sent to Ellis and the chairman of the managers in a private letter.

Education Welfare Officer Margaret Bray, a newcomer to the area, visited the school on February 4th. She indicated she had heard at Divisional Office that the staff were an International Socialist cell. Yet no Tyndale teacher was a member of any political party. That such statements were circulating within ILEA offices indicates the pernicious and insidious nature of the political rumour-mongering of the previous months.

The music therapy project had been set up permanently within the school. Robert Hamilton and Ezekiel Yearwood, two professional steel band musicians, made a set of tuned steel drums on site, helped by the children: this was a relevant and exciting

84

experience. (Hart complained, again without informing Ellis, about the bonfire Hamilton and Yearwood made in order to tune the drums.) The players were beginning to show expertise, and what had begun as therapy now began to develop into a musical venture of high standard and great possibilities.

The school was fostering further links with the community. The children went regularly to the local sports centre and the Islington Boat Club, essential recreational outlets in a borough which boasts two prisons but no substantial green space. There were a large number of visits, and the yearly school journey to Norfolk was reaching the final stages of preparation.

The psychotherapy unit was developing. Close contact was being maintained between the school and the local remedial reading teacher, who was often in the building, gave advice and supplied material. The ILEA Educational Welfare Officer was a frequent visitor, and Ellis spent many hours discussing problems of both children and parents.

Tyndale was achieving a cohesion and unity of purpose that would have seemed impossible a year before. The children were responding to the fresh teaching approaches. The possibilities for the future seemed bright. But outside the 'hawks' were gathering in increasing numbers.

Chapter 8
The Managers

The poor showing of the managing body at the inquiry, and their probable inability to keep open the school they have so desperately fought over, was a failure in the exercise of political opportunism. Finding themselves opposed to the political stances and educational practices of the staff, the managers made early attempts to influence a change of direction in the progress of the school. When these failed, they saw their only effective measure was to change the regime. They had to remove Ellis, and in doing so needed the aid of ILEA.

By July 1974, two terms after Ellis' appointment, the secret meeting at Divisional Office had effectively placed him on probation. By February 1975 Hoodless told Truman the managers wanted re-organization, with Hart in control. ILEA failed to act and, frustrated by their impotence to affect the running of the school, the managers came into conflict with the authority.

Managers have recently been encouraged by the ILEA to participate more in the schools. Courses in school management have been organized, to educate them in their role. However, through the indefinable nature of the rules of management, this participation can only operate when there is no conflict. The 'grey areas' mean managers are powerless to take effective action against schools they dislike unless the authority is willing to support them. Not only did ILEA fail to support the Tyndale managers, they also acted in a way interpreted as obstructive.

The managers and their connections found information difficult to obtain from the ILEA bureaucracy. In September 1975 Page complained to the leader of Islington Council ' I do think the Authority makes unnecessary trouble for itself by not conducting its affairs sufficiently openly . . . Many matters are discussed only between Chairman and Chief Officers, which then only gets conveyed by informal means. No automatic consideration of local membership or representation is ever given when plans are being laid . . . This is why I go along with those who say that to get information out of the Authority is hard — it is hard as a Member, harder still outside.'

The background of political hostility between the County Hall old guard of the Labour Party and the young, middle-class Labour Party members in Islington may have been a further motivating factor in the actions of some managers. Tennant believed the ILEA bureaucracy was unwieldy and ineffectual, run by 'failed politicians'. The Islington Education Advisory Committee was to be set up in July 1975 in order to improve, amongst other things, the supply of information from ILEA. ILEA retaliated at the height of the conflict by instructing its officers not to co-operate with the Advisory Committee. Devolution of educational power was becoming a serious consideration in Islington.

Given the encouragement of greater managerial involvement and the desire for local borough control, it is not surprising that the politically astute amongst the Tyndale managers saw the dispute, ostensibly over 150 children's education, as a means of raising wider issues. However, they waged their campaign so deviously and inconsistently that their credibility and effectiveness were disastrously impaired.

For Labour-Party-appointed managers to consort with Black Paper campaigners, and eventually vote to 'lock out' from their place of work fellow members of the Labour movement, is a most politically expedient act. However, it is not unusual for the Labour Party to behave in this way, though usually without such disastrous consequences. Indeed, ILEA were equally opportunistic in their handling of the affair. Opportunism fails when it is exercised without power.

Not all authorities have separate managing bodies for individual schools; even in London church schools differ in their method of appointing managers. Wiliam Tyndale Junior and Infant Schools have a managing body of nineteen:

1 Seven political appointments by the majority authority, ILEA.
2 Five political appointments by the minor authority, Islington Borough Council.
3 Two parents, one junior, one infant, elected by parents attending a meeting convened for that purpose.
4 Two assigned teachers, elected separately by the permanent teaching staff of each school.
5 One nominee of the University of London Institute of Education.
6 The head teacher of each school.

The body serves for four years, the duration of each Greater London Council. Parent managers are only eligible whilst their children are at the school, and teacher managers whilst employed there. The party complexion of the political appointments depends upon the balance of the parties on both the GLC and the local borough council. The Tyndale managers had only one Conservative member, and were therefore capable of being controlled by Labour Party policies.

Managers must hold at least one meeting a term, though any two managers or the chairman may summon one at any time. The constitution and conduct are governed by the 'Instrument of Management' as laid down in the 1944 Education Act. Conduct in relation to the running of the school is governed by the authority in its separate 'Rules of Management'. Both the Instrument and the Rules are to be found in 'the green book', given to all managers and assigned teachers on appointment. Officially the Chief Education Officer is clerk to every managing body, but the job is delegated to the Divisional Officer, who in turn delegates it to a team of clerks.

In most London schools managing bodies are peripheral organizations, making little attempt to influence schools. Generally they are used as a rubber stamping mechanism for the arrangements made between head teachers and Divisional Office. These may be of a professional nature with the District Inspector, or an administrative nature with the Divisional Officer. Indeed McColgan, a teacher with over twenty years' classroom experience, had never, before Tyndale, met a manager in her classroom. Whilst teachers were speaking at schools during the strike, they found a large proportion of staffs needed explanations of what managers were and how they functioned. This lack of identifiable purpose in school management is reflected both in the difficulties faced by political parties in recruiting managers, and in the poor attendance at meetings held to elect parent-managers.

The Tyndale staff were opposed to 'sleeping' managers, and tried to involve them in the running of the school. Many attempts were made to co-operate with those managers showing a constructive interest. Initially all managers had free access to classrooms without appointment. Only Chowles opposed this, specifically objecting to what she saw as Dewhurst's interference.

It was Ellis who introduced to managers' meetings more precise and detailed reports on the school, and first noted the progress of the roll at the top of reports. Never before had Tyndale's managers had so much information and freedom. The staff's libertarian attitudes towards them, and ILEA's token attempts to encourage greater involvement, offered a chance to the managers to test their powers of influence.

Managing bodies are regarded as sub-committees of ILEA, and all resolutions passed go to County Hall for consideration. If the relevant ILEA members choose to ignore these resolutions they have the power to do so. Thus managing bodies are dependent for action on County Hall policy. The Tyndale affair touched crucial facets of managerial 'powers', and underlined the point that managing bodies who assert themselves without the backing of County Hall are impotent.

Managers have most influence on a school over staff appointments. The procedure for head teacher appointments can be used as a tactic for controlling a school. From a short list of original applicants managing bodies must nominate three for interview by the Staff and General Sub-Committee of the ILEA. Whilst they are able to be represented at the final interview and indicate a preference, the final decision lies with the sub-committee. In 1974 managers at Highbury Grove School, also in Islington, refused to nominate any candidates for interview at County Hall. They feared the ILEA would appoint a candidate they did not want, and thus refused to send any forward. Amid controversy the post was re-advertised, and a candidate acceptable to the managers appointed. At Tyndale in July 1973 a similar situation arose over the appointment of a new head. It is speculation, but one must suggest that had Tyndale not been in such a difficult situation, the managers may have similarly refused to nominate on readvertisement in November 1973.

Managers have the power to appoint assigned and responsibility-posted teachers. It would be rare for them not to appoint if the head showed a preference for one candidate. At Tyndale some managers toyed with the idea of not appointing anyone for the scale 2 post taken up by Austin. Fairweather told Ellis and Haddow that a group of managers had met and considered 'not appointing anyone, in case the staff got someone they wanted'.

Influence through the appointment procedures is severely limited however, as the authority retains the final decision in the case of heads. The non-appointment of other staff is such an unsubtle hindrance that the resulting 'bad blood' would create a conflict which, without authority backing, managers have no power to control.

The two greatest controversies concerning managerial rights in the Tyndale case were over curriculum control and right of access to the school. Managers' control over the internal running of schools is ambiguously referred to in the authority's Rules of Management: 'the managers shall, in consultation with the head teacher, exercise the oversight of the conduct and curriculum of the school'. They go on: 'subject to the provisions of these rules, the head teacher shall control the conduct and curriculum, the internal organization, management and discipline of the school'. The vagueness of the concepts of 'oversight' and 'control' make these rules meaningless, and inapplicable when put to the test in a conflict. It can be argued that this is deliberate. Mabey's written evidence to the inquiry illustrates this point. He states: 'In relation to the authority I believe that in part the problems have arisen because of the authority's reluctance to indicate adequately what it expects from primary schools, and because of the confusion which exists about the control of the organization and curriculum.' He points out that the model articles of management in a government White Paper clearly define the tripartite functions of Authority, Management and head teacher. In paragraph 8(a) they state: 'the Governors shall have the general direction of the conduct and curriculum of the school', and in 8(b) 'subject to the provisions of these Articles the head master shall control the internal organization, management and discipline of the school.'

Mabey concludes his evidence in a penetrating manner. 'The authority's Rules of Management however blur this clear distinction by inserting a paragraph 2(a) the phrase "in consultation with the head teacher" and in 2(b)"shall control the conduct and curriculum". I have been unable to discover why the authority did not follow the advisory Rules of Management. I believe this conscious fudging of responsibility has been an important cause of the present dispute. What in effect we have is the authority saying nothing about general policy and leaving it to the local level, but where that responsibility rests then, there is more than a degree of confusion.'

When rules are ill-defined, those with power can intervene when they wish and 'clarify' rules, which they can then claim have been broken. Leila Campbell, a member of ILEA's Schools Sub-committee, when asked at a meeting of Islington managers and governors about the 'grey areas' of curriculum control, was aghast that well-meaning people should need written rules. She indicated that the present situation gave individuals more freedom within the management system. She failed to say it also gave the authority more freedom 'to play the system'. Within ILEA managers have no control over the curriculum unless the head so allows it; or, if the managers are in conflict with the head, the authority accepts managerial opinion, and intervenes.

The issue of right of access to a school was raised in the Tyndale dispute, and its lack of precedent had GLC and Islington Borough lawyers chasing around trying to uncover who had rights where. It became clear that individual managers do not have automatic access to a school building or classroom. They cannot come in at will or even by appointment, if the head finds this inconvenient or unacceptable. The only statutory right of access is for a managing body to delegate one of its members at a properly convened meeting to visit the school, and presumably report back to the next convened meeting. Hinds was to put it thus: 'my personal view is that no individual member has rights or duties to inspect. By analogy, under Standing Orders of the Council, no member of the Council may visit or has the right or the duty to visit a site belonging to the GLC and demand to see the ways in which the staff are performing on that site, but on the other hand a committee responsible for the work of a department can organize an official visit by 5 or 6 members of the committee. I think it is open to question whether any individual manager has a right to enter specified classrooms.'

Naturally this red tape is generally cut through, but it is clear managers only have a corporate right of access to a school at a time deemed convenient to those working in it.

Managers do have a limited power over ILEA policy in the authority's complex disciplinary procedures. Following the Houghton strike, the Tyndale teachers were warned by Briault that a repetition of their unofficial action would result in an investigation by the managing body, presumably to establish whether a *prima facie* case existed to justify a disciplinary tribunal. Although this never occurred, several teachers in London were placed before their managers. In each case the managers ruled that there was no charge to answer, thus thwarting ILEA's intentions.

Managers may make complaints to the authority about a head or a teacher's conduct, as was possible over Walker, and was to happen over the strike in September 1975. However, it is left to the authority's discretion in such a case whether disciplinary procedures are instituted. The Rules of Management clearly state that the termination of a head teacher's or assistant teacher's engagement is reserved to the authority.

Hinds has said the authority relies on adults behaving as adults— leaving teachers to teach, managers to manage. But what they teach and manage is confused. Managers are in an impossible position: encouraged to participate, told they are responsible for the school, they are given almost no power to do anything about the institution. Have they any value in the authority's system, beyond providing a benign facade of local participation?

Managers can be expected to fight for influence, which is what the Tyndale managers chose to do—struggle against a situation of responsibility without power. Prior to the findings of the Taylor Committee looking into School Management, which may change their status, managers have only two possibilities. Either they become authority hacks rubber-stamping ILEA policy, or they operate a guerilla action outside the rules, relying on public opinion to change that policy—an action to which any group may resort.

The Tyndale managers were mainly young, middle-class emigrés settled in the owner-occupier ghettos of Barnsbury, part of the 1960s renovation of Islington. They were not reflective of the mass of children who attended the school. Major factors in their later actions were their political connections and their associations with the media. All but one of the political appointments were in the patronage of the Labour Party; seven were card-carrying members.

They were experienced school managers, several being long-serving members of other bodies. The final composition included five chairmen or former chairmen of managing bodies, one councillor, the chairman of the Islington Trades Council, the wife of the deputy leader of Islington council, the wife of a council alderman, and the secretary of Page's ward constituency party—all articulate people familiar with political infighting. It is rumoured that several local figures were queueing up for a place on the Tyndale body.

It is difficult to ascribe a composite view to their political and educational attitudes, but one can deduce that their educational philosophy was represented by Hart's Infant School, which they believed to be the paragon of 'progressive' education—a progressiveness favouring the middle classes, and strictly non-radical. Tennant once said he was in favour of 'a bourgeoisifying process for working-class children'.

The policy of the 'active' group was conventional Labour Party: against militant actions, and opposed to anything which might alienate the middle classes. It is hardly surprising that this thoroughly bourgeois body came in conflict with a staff Tennant believed to be 'anarchistic'.

The actual dispute centred around the educational philosophy and the 'trade union' stances of the teachers. It was exacerbated by a series of inconsistent and opportunistic managerial actions which led to the final cataclysm.

By July 1974 the staff's actions over the London Allowance campaign, the employment of McColgan, and their policy of positive discrimination in favour of the disadvantaged, had sown the seeds of political doubt in the minds of some managers. With help from Walker and Buxton, they became convinced the staff were politically motivated in an extreme left direction, and that the school was not going to cater for the whole social range of children. Mabey wrote of the June 13th strike meeting: 'What was also clear was that the teachers were attempting to use the parents, as they had previously used the managers, to further wider objectives.' Tennant described the staff walk-out on July 9th as a 'political act', and Burnett, after seeing the steel band, noted that the school was not catering for the whole social range.

It may well be that schools *should* cater for all children; in London they do not and cannot. School and social conditions make it impossible. All teachers have a choice of where to lay the emphasis in classes, which group will get the time and attention. The vast majority opt for the privileged children. But Tyndale had set its priorities, and the managers recognized its danger.

From autumn 1974 the battle lines were drawn. The managers were committed to removing Ellis and breaking up the school's regime. The staff were committed to a defence of their beliefs, their place of work, and their children. Had the managers made their fight a principled one, based on a consistent ideological difference with the staff, they may well have come out of the battle with honour. However, they fought in a devious and clandestine fashion. Secret petitions, meetings behind closed doors and press leaks are the actions of those refusing to express their convictions openly. This is best demonstrated by the managers' attitudes in three crucial areas: strikes, parents and education.

In January 1974 Haddow, as staff representative, asked the managing body for support of action designed to secure an increased London Allowance. They gave it. In June 1974 they were asked for a renewal of that support. Haddow was told he could not have 'a carte blanche to go on strike'. In February 1975, having been threatened by ILEA with disciplinary action over the Houghton strike, Haddow inquired whether the Labour Party managers would put trade unionists on trial for going on strike. Hoodless was non-committal. In September 1975 Tennant was to comment to Haddow and Ellis on separate occasions that if they were to strike the Tyndale issue would achieve national importance and their case be heard. Two weeks later Tennant chaired the meeting that made an official complaint against the teachers' action.

At the inquiry the managers were to espouse the cause of parents' rights. However, on the subject of transfer to secondary school, they resolved on July 15th 1974 that 'the managers of William Tyndale school favour the discontinuing of banding and recommend the abolition of parental preference, with no opting out'. Their concern for parents can be demonstrated by their attitude to Newman, the parent-manager for 1974-5, and a staff supporter. His election was opposed, and he was excluded from the meetings with Hinds in early 1975. Perhaps the greatest insult to him was in September 1975, when he handed a statement to the managers' meeting in support of the teachers' strike, criticising Chowles for 'blacklegging' and hitting children. Mabey's reaction was to ask for Newman's union number, in order to report his conduct to the Transport and General Workers Union. It seems the parents were right as long as they were on the right side.

The managers' attitude to educational philosophy is perhaps the most striking. The supporters of a 'progressive' Infant School were to find themselves endorsing Chowles, an admitted supporter of Walker. The early contacts with Walker and her 'Black Paper' are also mystifying: why should an acknowledged left winger, such as Gittings, secretly associate with right-wing Black Paperism? The way in which they supported the methods used in the school during the periods covered by the strike and the inquiry is also revealing. The school was to be run in a most formal manner. Parents reported cases of alleged staff violence to children. Yet the managers in their meetings only made gestures of gratitude and admiration for the work undertaken by temporary staff.

To what extent was the school being used as a pawn in the battles Islington politicians were fighting? It cannot be an accident that the majority of Mabey's written evidence to the inquiry is a political diatribe on the powers of managing bodies. Someone with Tennant's views on ILEA would surely not be averse to devolution of educational power to the boroughs.

Even though ILEA operated a joint steering committee with Islington to discuss educational matters specific to the borough, Islington set up its own Advisory Committee in June 1975. Its chairwoman was Page and its membership included Mabey, Councillor David Hyams, who was involved in Hoodless' petition, and Councillor David Howell, expert on school management, managers' witness at the inquiry, Tyndale Infant parent, and advisor to Gittings during the conflict. The committee's terms of reference were exceptionally far reaching, and apparently a duplication of ILEA's function, being 'all matters relating to Education and the Education services'.

One of its chief concerns was the difficulty in ascertaining information from ILEA. At its first meeting it urged 'school managers, ratepayers or parents to seek out information about the existing education services, where the lack of information was apparent, for feeding back to the committee'. Was Islington witnessing the first rumblings of a devolutionary process of shifting educational power to the boroughs? Were school managers attempting to implement Islington Labour Party policies by circumventing central control, and influencing schools through their managerial status?

Ironically, Tyndale's teachers would agree with many aspects of the managers' case against ILEA, and support a defining of the rules of management. They are not against a decentralization of educational bureaucracy, nor a greater involvement of the local community in schools. Where they opposed their managers was in defence of their ideals, and their right to work in their chosen way. Where they criticized them was in their attitudes towards society, and their means of waging the battle.

Chapter 9
April – July 1975

The summer term began calmly. In early April in a letter to Hinds, Page was still pressing for an inspection, suggesting it was time for Michael Birchenough, ILEA chief inspector, to 'send in his troops'. Her letter also expressed the hope that the managers would pursue their anxieties through the managing body, and urged Hinds to 'grasp the nettle' of the North London Teachers' Association. She obviously considered he feared conflict with the union, whose local branch had a militant reputation. She herself feared that 'public involvement' would soon be invoked.

On April 9th the General Management Committee of the South Islington and Finsbury Labour Party, most of whom had never been near Tyndale, received the St Mary's Ward resolution. On April 25th Hinds received a letter from Hoodless. She drew his attention to an article she had read about 'headteachers of a certain kind' being moved sideways, and told him 'we are well forward with our petitions'. He did not react. On April 28th Hoodless started the petition on its career—round the governing body of the secondary school where she was chairwoman.

It read:

'We, the undersigned, are concerned at the deteriorating quality of education at William Tyndale Junior School, and note the rapid decline in the roll at a time when neighbouring schools are full, and call upon the ILEA to take urgent steps to re-establish public confidence in this junior school.'

This petition ran like a thread through events, until it was presented to the ILEA Schools Sub-committee on July 15th. It was to be circulated by many individuals besides Hoodless—Fairweather, Gittings and Burnett, Gittings' friend Hercules, local councillors Pedrick and Hyams (the latter a primary school teacher), and Jane Howell, wife of the councillor on the Islington Educational Advisory Committee.

When asked at the inquiry why no attempt was made to circulate it among the parents of Tyndale children, Hoodless said secrecy was necessary in order not to alarm these parents. Yet the petition had been circulated in the first place because Hoodless claimed parents were worried; it was simply a way of 'proving' this to Hinds. Later she claimed many parents disliked the school, and only kept their children there because they were unaware of their right to move them. The petition was circulated in June among parents of Infant School children. The aim was not so much to conceal it from the parents, as to keep it hidden from the teachers. The fatuousness of this is demonstrated by the fact that, on the first day of its circulation, the Junior staff heard of it through schoolkeeper Campbell. On April 29th came the rumour that Hoodless and Pedrick were involved.

The staff were about to discuss plans for the following year. They could not act on what were, for the moment, only rumours. Haddow had produced a discussion paper for the staff meeting of April 30th, intended to provoke thought and argument, and containing radical educational ideas. The opening paragraph reflected the militancy and resentment aroused in the staff by rumours of a new attack on the school.

At an Islington council meeting on May 12th, Pedrick informed Mabey of the petition. On the 15th, Mabey had a meeting at his house with Hoodless and Fairweather who, in Tennant's absence, was to chair the managers' meeting of May 19th. These three worked out a strategy for that meeting. Mabey had placed an item about the falling roll on the agenda. The figures provided by ILEA were arranged so that it was not made clear the fall had been arrested. This, together with the petition, was to be put to the managers as

98

the basis for the following resolution, to be proposed by Mabey and seconded by Hoodless:

'We the managers of William Tyndale School note with concern:
1. The petition circulating in the neighbourhood about the Junior School.
2. The rapidly declining rolls.
We call upon the ILEA to take urgent steps to restore public confidence in the schools, including consideration of re-organization as a JM and I school.'

That same week, Fairweather visited the school to discuss the forthcoming managers' meeting with Ellis and Haddow. She hoped they were not intending to raise any contentious matters. Haddow feared attacks on the school might be boiling up again, and put to her the petition rumours. She made no comment, even though she must have known of it, having been at the discussion in the ILEA Members' bar after the March 26th meeting. Ellis and Haddow recall Fairweather's visit taking place after May 15th, which meant she must have known about the plan concocted for the managers' meeting.

Mabey visited the school on May 16th, again without appointment. As a number of teachers were on a school journey, and Ellis was teaching full time, he told Mabey it was not convenient for him to see classes. Mabey left. He maintained later that 'Had the head been more welcoming' he would have discussed the petition and resolution. But he did not.

The managers' meeting of May 19th finally provoked open conflict. First, the head's report was attacked. The exciting ventures the school were undertaking were treated in a dismissive manner. Even the achievement of the Steel Band was ignored, though it had been selected for the ILEA 'In Pursuit of Excellence' exhibition.

Next, the item about the roll was brought forward. Ellis' request for a special meeting to discuss it was rejected, on the grounds that the matter was urgent. But if speed was the essence, why had Hoodless and her associates waited so long to hold a managers' meeting?

Even now they were not making a direct complaint about the running of the school.

Having suggested the roll was falling, Mabey produced a blank copy of the petition, which was used to convince the other managers of widespread local discontent. Had they known that some of their own number had started the petition which they were now being invited to 'note with concern', their reaction might have been different. At the inquiry, manager John Bolland expressed his disapproval of it, but at the meeting neither he nor most of the other managers were given correct information about it. Mabey deliberately avoided divulging all he knew; Ellis' questions were effectively suppressed by Fairweather in the Chair; and neither she nor Hoodless volunteered information about their part in what was going on. The air of shadowy intrigue was heightened by the fact that the blank petition contained no note of its originators. Nor did Mabey produce any evidence that anybody had signed it.

Ellis and Haddow tried to get the resolution amended, to ask the ILEA to investigate the reasons for the declining roll. When this was lost, the managers passed the resolution. The wording was based on incomplete information; at least half the resolution came from an alleged petition of which most managers had no knowledge; and those who were in a position to enlighten them consciously held back because they had set the whole thing up in the first place. It was a classic instance of the manipulation of a public body.

The suggestion about re-organization made on February 27th had at last achieved the status of a resolution; Ellis was quick to see the threat to his own position. Mabey certainly believed that this was now in question.

Mabey later admitted that the introduction of the petition at the meeting had probably been a 'tactical' mistake. It certainly had. The staff now knew it existed, and Mabey's possession and concealment of it linked it to both the managers and the local Labour Party. Confirmation came the next day with the news that Pedrick was circulating it. But Tyndale parents who were asked by the teachers still knew nothing; nor did the NUT representatives at local schools, who were contacted by McWhirter.

The teachers were still willing to use the proper channels of communication to put their case. In a letter of May 20th they urged Hinds and Bramall to reject the resolution, investigate the source of the petition, and meet a deputation. Hinds could not act because he was away on leave; in his absence, nobody else bothered.

Tennant, back from Africa, visited the school on May 21st and 22nd. He claimed no prior knowledge of the resolution, but generally approved it, and said if the staff sent him statements about it, he would throw them in the waste-paper basket. He believed the manager/teacher conflict had reached a level where a third party should intervene.

Ellis telephoned Rice, and received assurances that there were no plans for re-organization. But, as the efficiency of the school had been called into question by the resolution, on May 23rd Ellis wrote to Rice for further professional reassurance and guidance, urging him to come to the school as soon as possible. Yet, apart from a hurried visit to the dining-hall, which the staff never knew about, Rice stayed away until September 24th.

In spite of the consternation caused by the resolution, the school, in an educational sense, was going well. Another successful school journey had been led by Green. The Steel Band was giving concerts in other schools, in preparation for the ILEA exhibition. Caryl Harter and Joan Mills of the Royal Court Theatre were working regularly with children on an improvised play. Much effort was being expended on the preparations for the Community Carnival. Links had been established with Paddington College of Further Education, and a joint film-making project had been planned with lecturers and students.

Soon after the May resolution McWhirter, the school's NUT representative, contacted the Union's regional official Horace Perrin, seeking his advice. Perrin did not visit the school until six weeks later. On May 29th she wrote to Pedrick, requesting information about the petition. He replied on June 5th: 'I don't like the tone of this letter, and I suggest to you that if it's information you want you find it yourself; any other letters from you along this line will not be answered by me.' He regarded her letter as a threat, and, fearing legal action from the teachers, stopped his activities. But if the petition was in the public interest, contained nothing defamatory, and was not canvassed with malicious intent, what had he to fear? A feature of the petition was the secrecy with which its originators and circulators acted. The managers later claimed it was an example of democracy in action.

On June 2nd the NLTA gave the teachers strong support, calling on members to oppose the entry into their schools of children withdrawn from Tyndale. This 'locking-in' of children so incensed Burnett, who had been 'inactive' since giving up the Chair, that she obtained a copy of the petition and canvassed it among her friends, most of whom knew nothing about Tyndale.

Hinds was now grappling with the conflict. As the first step towards a solution, he met Tennant on June 16th. Again, managers were to put their case first. Hinds apparently envisaged inspectorial support for the school to allay the managers' anxieties, although Tennant did not believe such measures would clear matters up.

Much discussion in the inquiry centred around Tennant's description of some teachers as 'anarchistic'. Tennant tried to assert that he meant the school was chaotic. But Hinds' personal assistant, Sandra Horsfall, affirmed in evidence that she interpreted the word to refer to alleged 'outside activities'. Hinds himself was later to tell the teachers he had not been aware of any political 'smears' until Tennant's visit.

Tennant wrote to Hinds on June 18th, asserting his lack of confidence in the measures ILEA had proposed. Since the staff had requested that ILEA receive a deputation nearly a month before, and none of them had even been invited to this meeting, they began to feel the ILEA was siding with the managers.

The idea of a community carnival had been suggested the previous term. The staff wished to create a genuine local event, rather than the usual school fair whose main concern is making money. Local organizations and charities were invited to take part, as was the Infant School. The Juniors' resisted the Infants' idea that an entrance charge should be made, feeling the main purpose was to get as large an attendance as possible, and convince local people the school was an important part of their community. The carnival, held on June 7th, was a great success, and was supported by the ILEA community relations inspectorate, which obtained a grant from the Islington Council. While the Junior staff were working hard in the playground to make this venture a success, Hoodless conducted herself on a tour of the Junior building.

On June 19th the Steel Band appeared at County Hall at the exhibition organized by Pape. These children, many of whom would have been classified elsewhere as extremely difficult, performed in front of an enthusiastic audience of teachers, parents and inspectors.

Still trying every avenue, the staff contacted local MP George Cunningham on June 11th. He invited them to his 'surgery' on June 20th, but informed Tennant of their request. The teachers arrived early. Tennant, Hoodless, Fairweather and Burnett were just leaving the Labour Party rooms. The interview with Cunningham was not characterised by politeness on his part. He objected to McColgan's attempt to take a short note, and when the staff complained they were accused of being an extreme 'left' group, his only remark was, 'Well, are you?' He said there was nothing he could do to help, and that the staff would have to find someone who would 'listen to them'. His view was expressed later to the House of Commons, where he gave a summary of what he called the 'facts' of the Tyndale affair, which was an exact summary of the managers' view.

The staff's move to direct action came on the occasion of a proposed visit by Gittings. On June 20th she discussed various matters with the teachers. She told them the petition had been started by Pedrick; the time had come for the managers to act; standards at the school had been declining since 1972; and (although her criteria were purely subjective) she wished to visit classes to make a judgement about them. She was asked to return on the 23rd.

The staff felt it important to consider carefully a response to managers' attempts to assess what was happening in classrooms. It seemed obvious that, since the resolution of May 19th was tantamount to a vote of no confidence, any managerial visit could only involve a search for evidence to re-inforce and give credence to that resolution. Besides Gittings, Tennant and Mabey were already 'booked' for visits. It was decided, therefore, to exclude managers from the school in working hours. On June 23rd a statement of exclusion was issued, giving reasons, and only agreeing to see managers before or after school. Gittings complained to ILEA and, with Hercules, started canvassing the petition among Infant parents.

The 'access' question was open, and Mabey was the first to put it to the test. ILEA were anxious for him not to visit the school, fearing an escalation of the conflict. He was equally determined to test his rights, and carry out his responsibilities as he saw them. On June 27th, with Fairweather, he met Ellis in his room. In the presence of McWhirter, Mabey asked to see 'if the children are being taught properly' — which was a demand to inspect the school. He was excluded. He complained to ILEA, and consulted the Islington Council solicitor about his rights. ILEA declined to secure him access; the solicitor could only report that there was no clear way through the question. On June 30th Tennant and Hoodless were refused admission to classes.

The managers now hit back, and in doing so pushed the troubles of Tyndale into the public arena which it never afterwards left. Burnett, Tennant, Hoodless, Fairweather and Mabey met to plan a set of notes to distribute to the press. These were based on the 'information' Hoodless had collated for the County Hall meeting in February. The general public thus got its first impression of the school from the questionable material supplied by those actively working against its staff, who were willing to subject them to untold pressure to achieve their ends.

Ellis and Haddow had already complained to Fairweather, without any response, about Mabey's concealment of the petition. They now complained to ILEA about his conduct and that of Gittings, who had been seen by Arnold outside the school, canvassing the petition while trying to keep it hidden in a library book. ILEA seemed to have lost the initiative. To regain it, Hinds set up a meeting at County Hall. He invited all Junior staff and all the managers, and Hart and the Infant teacher-manager Angela Jay. This round-table conference was intended to thrash matters out and seek a solution.

On the morning of this conference the material released by the managers was published in *The Times*. Burnett had been in contact with this newspaper on June 30th, and the article quoted both Mabey and Tennant. It mentioned educational incompetence and the determination of the curriculum on political grounds. Other newspapers took these matters up.

The teachers went to County Hall under the worst possible circumstances, but believing that at last they were going to be able to put their case. But the room was full of officials, including · the head of TS13, the ILEA disciplinary department. With complaint and counter-complaint already in front of ILEA, Hinds announced that it was essential not to prejudice possible disciplinary proceedings by discussing matters which might properly come before a tribunal. Since it appeared ILEA had no procedure for dealing with complaints by teachers against managers, such a tribunal could only be directed against the teachers. This announcement stopped all details of the staff's case from coming out, and there were doubts about whether the meeting could continue. The Junior staff withdrew, but were advised by NUT official Perrin and NLTA secretary Smith to carry on.

Meanwhile the managers had been in discussion. According to Tennant, Jay suggested an inspection of both schools by the Department of Education and Science. Hart and the managers approved of the idea, and it was immediately put to the returning Junior staff, with the suggestion that it should be a joint managers'

104

and teachers' proposal. All discussion now centred round this. Hart accepted on behalf of her staff without consulting them. Attempts by Ellis, Haddow and McColgan to raise other issues were thwarted.

This proposal was a clever manoeuvre. If the teachers agreed, they would open themselves to investigation and the managers would successfully evade it; if they refused, it would seem they had something to hide. The managers were most concerned with the future, which, when one considers what some of them had been up to in the past, was not surprising. It was also noticeable that they still did not request an ILEA inspection. Ellis asked if they had consulted Rice. There was no answer.

Hinds had doubts about the speed at which an inspection could be mounted, even an ILEA one. Three months was thought to be a minimum period. He led everybody to believe that an inspection, either by ILEA or the DES, would look into the relationship between the school and its managers. This was not true; as an experienced ILEA   Member he should have known that.

Mabey was insisting the access question be resolved. But it had been suggested that no manager had individual rights, except when properly delegated by the corporate body. It was finally agreed the Junior staff should have a week to decide about the managers' proposal and, if they agreed, Hinds would request the Secretary of State to authorize an inspection of both schools. Hinds undertook to visit the school on July 8th to hear the staff's case.

On July 7th the NLTA overwhelmingly supported the staff in their exclusion of the managers.

Ellis and Haddow now wrote to Tennant, requesting information about statements made by managers in the newspapers, and the furnishing of background notes to the press. He never replied. He had already been quoted in the press as saying the managers supported the school but not some of its teachers. Yet the teachers are a vital ingredient of a school, and must be supported by the managers — unless those managers want them removed. Just to support the 'school' in such circumstances is to support the idea of educational provision on a particular site. It later became apparent this was precisely the position of certain managers — keep Tyndale in being, but get rid of certain staff.

With Hinds' visit on July 8th, the staff at last got their chance to state their case. He had been lending his ear to the managers and their political associates since June 1974. This was the first time he heard of many of the matters the staff considered relevant—above all, the political aspects.

Despite the request for information he had made in June 1974, Hinds seemed to know little about the Walker affair and the early attacks on the school. He had not even seen a copy of Walker's 'Black Paper'. The staff learned from him about Rice's March inspection, and the visits of certain female managers to County Hall, although the details remained secret.

The staff had prepared their case well, and gave Hinds the fullest information. But what steps could he now take? By patching up a compromise on July 2nd and agreeing to the DES inspection proposal, he had managed to divest ILEA of effective power. Nobody could do anything until the teachers replied; if that reply were negative, ILEA would be left with the same problem, except the circumstances would be less propitious, because of the time lost and the more aggressive positions the parties would have been forced into. The time to hear the teachers' case had been July 2nd. Instead, that conference had been used to set up a situation that led to a further conflict. July 8th was too late; the staff had been asking to be heard since September 1974.

The decision about the inspection had to be taken. Chowles, Buckton, Arnold and Austin were for acceptance. Ellis and the other six full-time teachers were against, since the proposal offered no prospect of what they wanted — an investigation of managers' actions since May 1974. The fact that, according to Hinds, Rice had found commendable aspects in the school only seemed to make the inspection more redundant. It was decided by the seven teachers that a negative answer should be sent to Hinds, and that Ellis and Haddow should put a motion to the managers inviting them to join the staff in asking the DES to investigate the management of the school. If this were rejected, they intended to contact the DES themselves, to request a full public inquiry.

At the managers' meeting of July 9th the teachers' proposal was rejected, and Bolland put a motion specifically requesting a DES inspection. Ellis sought an amendment asking for a separate investigation of the management. It was decided, however, simply to append the words 'the inspection should include teaching, administration and management'.

Many managers believed that this rider expressed their

willingness to have their own role investigated, and the staff were being intransigent in refusing to support it. But the teachers were aware that no inspectors could delve into the dangerous political areas of management. Anyway, how do you inspect a manager? Hinds would appear to agree with this view, when he wrote on July 11th that the managers' proposal 'would exceed the normal limits observed by Her Majesty's inspectors'. Yet he himself on July 2nd had led everybody to believe a DES inspection would consider management. Some managers were undoubtedly under a misapprehension about the business, so a formula acceptable to both sides was not found.

The access question was not considered. Tennant continued his dabbling with the press by taking the unusual step of inviting a journalist from *The Times Educational Supplement* to the managers' meeting.

On July 10th the seven teachers asked Hinds to reject the managers' resolution, pointing out that it was an attack on ILEA as well as them. The teachers asserted their claim for a DES inquiry into the activities of the managing body.

The same day a high-level meeting was held at County Hall between Bramall, Hinds and leading officials. It was here the ILEA inquiry was conceived. The managers' resolution was obviously aimed at ILEA.

If the DES were to intervene, ILEA would lose the initiative and find itself simply a party in a conflict (which both teachers and managers knew was the case anyway). To retain its power it now proposed to set up its own inquiry 'into the relations between managers and staff'. An inspection was to take place as soon as possible in the autumn term 'as part of the evidence to be submitted to the Inquiry'. This was an unprecedented use of an inspection, and was to be a prime cause of the explosion that took place in September. Inspections involve questioning teachers. How were they to answer, knowing they would appear before an inquiry later, but not knowing what that inquiry would demand of them? And how were inspectors to report, knowing their individual opinions might also be the subject of inquiry? There is evidence that some of those present at this meeting, later came to the view that the affair would be better settled by other means.

But any attempt at change would be pre-empted by ILEA's desire for a quick solution. This hurried proceeding was an attempt on ILEA's part to retain the initiative by any means. The teachers would get their inquiry and the managers their inspection. If either side failed to co-operate, it would seem to be masking its guilt. ILEA, controlling the procedure and timing of the inquiry, could perform its usual manipulative function, while masquerading as an honest broker.

Staff and managers were informed of the proposal on July 11th. Tennant was still exploring the DES option with Cunningham. On July 14th the staff responded by asking ILEA to counter the damage being done to the school by issuing a public statement of support. They requested a full public inquiry, and sent Hinds a copy of the submission they were making to the DES. Their contention to the Secretary of State was that 'the managing body has acted unreasonably and proposes to continue acting unreasonably'.

Ten separate matters with numerous sub-headings were submitted by the teachers, with a request for a full public inquiry to be set up by the DES. ILEA issued a press release setting out their inquiry proposals, and the staff did the same, putting forward their point of view, since ILEA made no statement of support for them.

On July 15th Page handed the petition, which she had received on the 7th from Donald Hoodless, to the ILEA Schools Sub-Committee. It had been circulating for ten weeks, and had amassed 198 signatures — hardly an indication of a deep swell of public concern. Although a few Infant parents had signed it, no Junior parent had. It contained the signatures of twenty-eight Labour councillors and forty-five school managers, most of whom had no connection with Tyndale. One person had signed it three times, others twice, some 'just to make up the numbers'. Councillor Chris St Hill had signed it while trying to secure money for Tyndale to run the community carnival.

The teachers, meanwhile, had been seeking information on the petition. It was vital that they augment their scanty knowledge of it and, above all, find out who had signed it. McWhirter wrote on July 13th to both Page and Donald Hoodless. Page tried to induce ILEA to release a copy to the staff, but without success. Hoodless refused information.

By now another petition was circulating. Sympathy with the staff, and the rumours she heard in the Infants', had convinced part-time Infant teacher Margaret Ford that some method of support should be organized for the Juniors'. Together with David Harter and some local teachers, she began the William Tyndale Junior School Support Campaign, and organized a petition to be circulated among parents and trade unionists. This was clearly identified as emanating from the support campaign, and bore Ford's address. It read:

'We the undersigned support the present staff of William Tyndale Junior School in the work they have been doing in the school, and wish them to continue to teach the children of Islington without harassment or interference from managers, local councillors, government inspectors or the ILEA Authorities.'

This petition was circulating for a little over two weeks and was handed to the Sub-Committee on July 22nd. It contained 165 signatures, including nearly 50 Junior parents. To put over the teachers' case, which was mostly going by default in the press, the Campaign distributed information leaflets in the area.

On July 10th the school held an open evening. A large group of parents examined their children's work, listened to the Steel Band, watched the play by the Royal Court group and the film by the Paddington students. It was a successful social evening.

Hinds' inquiry proposal was to be debated by the Sub-Committee on July 24th. Term ended on the 19th. The staff therefore went on holiday not knowing whether they would have to face inspection and inquiry the following term. The debate, however, was a mere formality. Birchenough was informing Pape on the 23rd of the inspection dates (22nd-30th September, with a report ready by October 6th). Rice, who would normally have led the team, was to be excluded, not by order of his superior, Birchenough, but by Bramall.

On July 21st, Haddow and McWhirter tried to obtain a copy of the petition from Hinds, but he refused to provide one.

The ILEA Schools Sub-Committee duly passed the proposal. Baker made sarcastic comments about the 'non-teaching' at the school, which she briefly visited in September 1974. Hinds thought the Inquiry would only last a few days. He was asked if he had sounded out the teachers and managers, but Bramall intervened, saying the Sub-Committee was not a negotiating body, and ILEA could run its own schools. Had he been able to see two months into the future, he might have taken a different view.

Chapter 10
The Inner London
Education Authority

Hinds concluded his written evidence to the inquiry by saying: 'I take the view that much that is of value in the English educational system derives from the involvement of a number of groups of adults — head teachers, teachers, parents, managers or governors and the local community which the school serves. The ILEA place great confidence and trust in all these groups of adults. The view I take and which I have consistently taken in this affair is that it is only when all efforts to avoid a breakdown have failed that positive intervention by the Authority is justified.' This statement demonstrates clearly the authority's attitude. Even at the inquiry. ILEA was claiming to be the honest broker in a dispute between managers, parents and teachers. They failed to accept any involvement in or responsibility for the fate of Tyndale; Hinds did not even list officers and members of the authority as adults having a valuable involvement in the English educational system. Yet ILEA were a major force in the events at Tyndale.

At the Inquiry it was agreed by managers, teachers, press and impartial observers that ILEA were largely responsible for the ruin of one of their schools. Their non-intervention had allowed a dispute to rage for over a year, resulting in teachers, managers and parents becoming beyond their control, and bringing a welter of damaging publicity. Why did they choose to operate this policy? At any stage they could have supported the Tyndale staff, and made a statement to reassure parents. (This would not have been unusual; Hinds, following the Tyndale affair, appeared on television to defend an East London comprehensive, after right-wing teachers had criticised in the press the running and performance of the school.) The ILEA could have supported the managers and instituted plans for re-organisation. The school rolls would have warranted it, and it would have been in line with ILEA policy.

Was the Authority afraid of a confrontation with either group, fearing publicity? We know of the antagonisms between Islington and County Hall; to what degree was ILEA afraid of the North London Teachers' Association? In April 1975 Page had written to Hinds: 'It may well be time for the NLTA nettle to be grasped'. Of course ILEA had no need to fear the NLTA. Its militancy had been stifled as much by the loss of local branch autonomy as by the appeasing policies of its 'moderate' General Purposes Committee and secretary. However it was revealed at the inquiry that Hinds was working on past information, believing the association to be Rank and File led. He may have baulked at this confrontation.

The authority may also have feared raising the 'McColgan spectre', and not wished to risk further accusations of victimisation.

In varying degrees these fears were held by the hierarchy at County Hall. Their inaction was in part due to lack of information, the ineptitude and size of the bureaucracy causing a breakdown in communication between local and central administrations. But something more positive was involved.

Large bureaucracies can be fertile ground for individual manipulators. Actions taken by some staff at Divisional Office 3 need to be justified. Members' policy at County Hall seems to have been to steer a middle course between what NLTA secretary Smith described as 'two most difficult groups of people', giving each enough rope to hang the other, whilst the administration stored up complaints from either side. Had the strike in September 1975 not blasted the gambit out of control, the ILEA final solution of inspection and inquiry could have been ideal. Whilst Birchenough's 'troops' could have found Tyndale's education unsuitable, a short internal inquiry controlled by the Sub-Committee could have dealt with managerial improprieties.

Temporarily, at least, this was the result. Following the inquiry, teachers and managers went into semi-retirement with little control over the school, whilst ILEA stumbled on, its main combatants Rice and Hinds still pursuing their duties. However, the authority suffered more adverse publicity than any other group. The responsibility for this lies in their under-estimation of the determination of a small group of mere primary school teachers. At every turn opposition was supposed to cave in, Ellis would have a breakdown, and all would be well. But it never happened. When Tennant warned Hinds of potential staff opposition to the ILEA package of inspection and inquiry, he replied: 'We shall have to persuade them then.' He didn't, and ILEA strategy blew up.

On the evidence ILEA made available to the inquiry one can only guess at the reasons for their policy. Vital witnesses from Divisional Office 3 refused to give evidence, the most senior officer and member at County Hall were not called. ILEA claimed there was no file on William Tyndale; yet 'William Tyndale File' was clearly written on many documents. Also, during the inquiry, they claimed the Hoodless petition had been lost. The ILEA machine lends itself to inefficiency and deviousness.

Most social services in the twelve Inner London boroughs which the ILEA covers are administered by the borough councils. However, education is controlled by the Inner London Education Authority, an autonomous body quite separate from the Greater London Council. Its far-reaching powers are provided for in the 1944 Education Act. It is the authority's duty 'to secure that there shall be available, for their area, sufficient schools for providing primary education, that is to say, full-time education suitable to the requirements of Junior pupils'. The authority's rules of management further state: 'The Authority is obliged to determine the general educational character of the school and its place in the Authority's system' and: 'A basic allocation of teachers and non-teaching staff shall be allocated by the education officer to each school, together with additional resources including a school allowance for materials, equipment, activities and amenities in accordance with the authority's approved standards'.

It is within the authority's power to decide the nature of schools within its area — their size, age range, sex make-up and, before government intervention, whether they should be selective. It is for them to decide which and how many teachers a school should have, and to allocate money to equip them. A local authority is only accountable to the regulations and instructions of the DES.

ILEA policy is decided by the committees of those GLC councillors elected by their borough councils to serve on ILEA. The political balance of power is decided not by the GLC, but by the balance of parties within the Inner London boroughs.

This policy is administered by paid officials at County Hall, led by the Chief Education Officer and his Assistant Education Officers. The administrative work is delegated to ten divisional offices in the boroughs, each presided over by a divisional officer. In normal circumstances schools have administrative dealings only at divisional level. Teaching staff applications are dealt with here, and classroom teachers rarely penetrate beyond it in their appreciation of the ILEA machinery. Chowles, for instance, had no idea who Hinds was, and was amazed to discover he was simply an elected councillor. This hierarchical distancing of centralised power can be a major factor in the control of teachers. Once this remoteness was broken in the Tyndale case, and teachers came in contact with their real bosses in summer 1975, the situation soon escalated out of control. It was no longer possible to contain discontent at a local level.

The education in schools is supposed to be monitored by the ILEA inspectorate, which is divided into central and local levels. The Chief Inspector, staff inspectors for primary and secondary schooling, and teams of subject inspectors, have offices at County Hall, whilst each ILEA division has two or three overstretched district inspectors, who have direct contact with schools, and are expected to have detailed knowledge of each. Rice had sixty-two schools in his charge, as well as courses to run and conferences to attend. It would be impossible for anyone, however talented, to cope with such an amount of work.

A recent ILEA survey showed that inspectors spend only 5% of their time in schools. In practice, before the Tyndale affair, inspectors were rarely seen in classrooms. Their role as far as schools were concerned was two-fold: firstly, a benign one, working as advisors, mainly to head teachers; secondly, as 'trouble-shooters', moving in on potentially difficult situations to protect the authority's image. In the aftermath of Tyndale ILEA plans to double its inspectorate at district level. Teachers may find the benign attitudes becoming more inquisitorial, with more attention being given to standards, work schedules and records.

The job of administering education in schools falls to the head and staff. All teachers, under their contracts, are at the beck and call of the head. The professional conduct of teachers is provided for under the authority's staff code; any reported contraventions are sent to a branch of County Hall called TS13. This department, which deals with the disciplining of teachers, is strangely named Teachers' Welfare. A file is kept on every teacher, which may be seen by the teacher concerned at will, a fact not known by most teachers, and not widely publicised by the authority. Certain teachers' files take longer to find than others, and some are classified with red or black dots. Tyndale staff have only met teachers who have been involved in some form of militant action classified in this way.

All children also have files kept on them at their school, and these are available for parents to see on request.

A schoolkeeper, secretary and meals assistants are provided by the authority, but each school can provide itself with more ancillary help out of the year's allowance. The proposal that Tyndale's ancillary workers should give evidence on behalf of Walker in the inquiry created a potentially embarrassing situation for all concerned. Fortunately this was averted when they were not in the end called. But this does not diminish the fact that ancillary workers had helped Walker in her 'Black Paper' campaign, and were the source of information used against the staff by inspectors in September 1975.

How then does the authority lay down principles on the educational content of schools? It does not: it leaves each school to decide that for itself. Peter Newsam, Deputy Education Officer, stated in reply to a letter from Mabey: 'It is for each school to decide its own curriculum, organisation and methods of teaching. The Authority does not lay down an overall policy on these matters but, as the question indicates, has to ensure that the education provided is suitable.' The Authority has a policy on the structure of education, but delegates its decisions on content to individual schools. The inspectorate can advise, but has no power to insist or demand that head teachers change their policy. Only a disciplinary charge can remove a head. A more likely means is for the rebel head to find his school closed or reorganised, as with Duane's Risinghill, and with the managers' attempt to remove Ellis.

How do the authority's inspectorate decide whether 'suitable' education is being provided? Such a vast organisation will encompass   114 a spectrum of teaching methods and degrees of competence. For example, not far from the 'unsuitable' William Tyndale, a school was teaching pounds, shillings and pence to its children long after decimalisation. In another local school the head was known to practise golf shots locked in his office, while the school proceeded merrily below. All London teachers could relate equally bizarre and amusing happenings. What is it that makes one school 'suitable' and another not?

There are the inspectors' own subjective standards. Being largely ex-head teachers, they will have worked their way up the ladder through conforming, and not drawing adverse attention to themselves. They will veer towards the authoritarian and conventional, in the mould of the Geddes 'Sir was winning' approach (see page 43). They are unlikely to have taught in a classroom for several years, some never in London at all. They may have never practised modern techniques such as team teaching.

The two principal inspectors in the Tyndale saga, Rice and Pape, had not taught for many years, and even then only outside a major urban area. Whilst there are exceptions, the inspectorate are often out of touch with modern problems, and defenders of the educational and social status quo. Rice, when asked at the inquiry how he knew that Tyndale was working better, replied that it was much quieter! However, performance in London is measured not in decibels, but in the amount of adverse attention a school receives. ILEA is less concerned with educational content, than with its public image. Schools that create adverse publicity are bad and receive bad inspection reports; those that 'don't make waves' wallow on.

The ILEA inspectorate knew very little about how Tyndale worked. Although Rice claimed, during the inquiry, that he visited the Tyndale schools at least a dozen times, the teachers know that he visited some of their classes only once, and others not at all. He told the inquiry that three visits were to the school dining room.

Pape wrote a most damaging report on the school, yet had never seen any teachers' work. Inspectors Geddes and Welch wrote long, emotional diatribes to condemn people they had never seen. Geddes concluded his report: 'I earnestly suggest that the absentee teachers should be replaced by more competent and caring colleagues.'

The only subject inspector who had seen the school prior to the September inspection was Music Inspector Preston. In July 1975 he wrote: 'I believe the Head has made entirely sound decisions over music in the school, given the present difficulty of finding music teachers.' Only five working weeks later he reported: 'I would regard the provision of music experience for all the children in the junior school as an important priority.' The change in tone is subtle, but significant. At the time of the September inspection, ILEA were receiving bad publicity because of the teachers' strike.

Prior to the strike, in nearly two years, the ILEA inspectorate paid little attention to Tyndale. Only two subject inspectors visited, and these only saw Ellis in his room. Hardly the attention one might expect for a school which some commentators have said 'came apart'.

During the inquiry Pape claimed he had instructed Rice to step up the level of inspectorial interest in the school. He produced a memo, allegedly sent to Rice in March 1975. It stated: 'I think your inspection of the school cannot but be beneficial to the teachers. It would seem to me that now it should be followed up by visits of your colleagues to give guidance in specialist subject areas which appear to be below par.' However, this memo was variously dated by Pape in his evidence as having been sent in October, April and March of 1975. The top copy was still in his possession, and Rice had no memory of it. Even assuming that Rice was mistaken, why did only the Music Inspector appear, and then at Ellis's request? How can a secret inspection be of value to teachers who know nothing at all about it?

In order to cater for some of its 'maladjusted' children, Tyndale set up a sanctuary and a steel band, both approved of and encouraged by the inspectorate. Rice admitted at the inquiry that one of these maladjusted children was catered for better at Tyndale than he could be at any special school They thrived and were well integrated. However, the inspectors' first report recorded that the school had created an unfair burden for itself in catering for such children. Welch said of the steel band: 'I doubt, in my ignorance, the therapeutic value of this activity. It is my professional and informed opinion that to miss the valuable time ostensibly intended for skills learning is hardly likely to improve the attainment of the children concerned.' (The child that Tyndale had catered so well for was to be later recommended for special schooling by the temporary staff, and at his case conference, which none of his former teachers were allowed to attend, Rice is reported to have said that his behaviour had 'stood out like a sore thumb'.)

116

The ILEA forbid corporal punishment in its primary schools. However anyone connected with London schools knows it is still widespread, and in certain schools a daily occurrence. Chowles stated openly in staff meetings that she believed in smacking children, and at the inquiry admitted to hitting a child. Rice, too, under cross-examination, had to admit that one of the inspectors, taking a class during the strike, had seized a child and shaken him, causing a parent to complain.

A blind eye is generally turned to these incidents, and cases are rarely reported. Yet after the inquiry Felton was to be summoned for interview with the Chief Inspector and Chief Education Officer, for allegedly interfering in the running of his school. His crime was to discuss with parents who approached him for advice the correct procedure concerning accusations of violence to pupils, and questions of transfer to special schools.

Whilst the inspectorate appear to operate according to such pragmatic considerations, with Tyndale they only did so in obedience to their political masters. The ILEA Members piped the tune, while the inspectors danced behind. At the inquiry Pape, his retirement imminent, gave the game away in an uncharacteristic outburst. When questioned on the reasons for leaving Rice out of the final inspection team, which in normal circumstances he would have led, Pape shouted: 'The buck shouldn't always rest with the inspectorate, it was Sir Ashley Bramall's decision'. All through the conflict inspectors were carrying out orders. Both the secret inspections made by Rice were carried out on Hinds' orders. The decision to inspect the school before the inquiry was a political one.

Pape and Birchenough were disturbed at the precedent of an inspection forming part of the evidence for a public inquiry. Following his pre-inspection visit to the school, Pape wrote to Birchenough with a suggestion that could have avoided the final explosion. 'Institute further discussion at the highest level with the managers and the junior staff. Proceed with an inquiry (public or private?) into relationships between the managers and the staff. Leave it with the inspectorate to be attentive to the school. Undertake that any subsequent written report on the work of the school which may be made to the Chief Inspector shall be issued to the staff and managers, and may be the subject of discussion at a managers' meeting with the inspectors present.'

117 This imaginative way out was ignored by the politicians, who

had made their decisions. Bramall was not going to allow ILEA to become a 'negotiating body'. Pape dutifully followed his orders. Three times in the ensuing months political decisions were to overrule the inspectors. At a high-level meeting called to discuss the outbreak of the strike an enraged Birchenough, his inspection disrupted, was thwarted again. The note of the meeting reads: 'The Chief Inspector hoped to take immediate disciplinary action, but it had been made clear by Sir Ashley and Mr Hinds that although it was extremely likely we would have to take strong disciplinary action in the future, we had to stand firm and await the findings of the inquiry before initiating action'. Political expediency had won.

Before the teachers returned to work, Pape wrote again, this time to Briault, offering advice on the future of the inspection: 'If the teachers return, the unscrambling of the present situation will be very confusing to the children. If the inspection from that point is then to relate to the erstwhile state of the school, then in my view at least two weeks will be required to allow it to return to anything like normality.' A week later Bramall told a worried delegation of managers; 'It is not for the teachers' benefit that we want them there, it is for ours that we will complete the inspection.' Pape's advice had been ignored, and he went on to write a further, highly critical report.

A note of another high-level County Hall meeting, which discussed the publication of the inspection reports, gives further evidence of the inspectors' subordinate role. It says Birchenough was most unhappy to discover that these two documents would be made public at the inquiry. He felt that this would prejudice future professional relations between inspectors and teaching staff, and wished to advise in the strongest possible terms against making the documents public. The Leader and Mr Hinds both emphasized that there could be no question of the reports not being made publicly available to the inquiry.' At the expense of future professional relationships, the political decision prevailed. The two inspection reports were made available at the inquiry, as well as the individual inspectors' reports.

The ILEA is ultimately responsible for the state of each of its schools. The shambles that William Tyndale had been reduced to by October 1975 must be laid at their door. Three facets of the Authority's make-up are to blame: the inherent poor communications of a large bureaucracy; its tendency towards a policy of closed government; and its understimation of the potential force of united groups of teachers.

The events of summer 1974 demonstrate the confusion that arises from poor communication. In June Page contacts Hinds, transmitting managerial concern over Tyndale. Hinds goes to the Assistant Education Officer in charge of Primary Schools, Patricia Burgess, and requests information. Burgess sends a memorandum to Rice, indicating that Hinds is worried and asking for facts. In July Rice makes a secret report on the school, which is factually incorrect and based on dubious source material. He sends this to Burgess, with copies to Birchenough and Pape. And there it rests. Hinds is never made aware of its contents; he is simply told that a parents' meeting is being held 'to ensure understanding between parents and teachers'. A secret report on a school is never shown either to the man requesting it, the teachers concerned, or the managers who are worried

Running parallel to this Kafka-like absurdity is the Walker affair. Walker goes to Rice and complains, amongst other things, that Haddow is indoctrinating his children. Rice ignores this serious charge, neither visiting Haddow nor asking for his comments. Haddow and McColgan then make separate complaints about political harassment, which are rushed to Divisional Office for action. D O file the complaints, and they never appear again. Rice sits out of the July 9th parents' meeting, watching a political vendetta in action, and a head vilified by a part-time teacher. Again no intervention. Subsequently the managers wish to discuss Walker's conduct, but the Divisional Officer forbids it, saying the matter is in County Hall's hands. He informs TS13 that the had has taken offence at Walker's 'Black Paper'. No mention is made of political complains or disrupted meetings.

Also sent to TS13 are five counter complaints by parents against Ellis. On this information TS13 reply to DO3, with incomplete recommendations—not just on what Ellis can do, but also on Walker's possible action against Ellis! TS13 also inform Burgess, who naturally takes it no further. DO report the incomplete information of Ellis' options back to the managers' meeting, and again frustrate discussion on Walker, as she is not present. Asked if she can be invited to attend the next meeting, DO say it would not be in order. Everybody is floundering in the dark, acting on misleading information.

In October, amid this confusion, Hinds, who it seems has been informed of nothing, makes two fallacious statements. He tells the staff there have been no complaints received against them, either at County Hall or Divisional Office level. And in reply to a question in the Education Committee, inquiring into the falling roll at Tyndale, he informs his fellow councillors that a loss of seventy-four children in one year is due to 'the substantial move of population out of the area'. Was the Education Committee really to believe Islington was becoming a ghost town?

Whilst these events reveal ineptitude and inefficiency, one must also query the motivation and reasoning behind what must have been deliberate choices about the supply of information. What isolated Tyndale from the support usually lavished on ILEA schools in difficulty? There is evidence that it was not an educational distinction. As late as June 16th 1975 Hinds told Tennant that 'any formal complaint made against the head and the staff would probably founder, because the educational standards achieved at the school were certainly no lower than elsewhere in the division'. As early as the secret DO meeting of June 23rd 1974, Rice and Buxton had described three Tyndale participants — Ellis, Haddow and McColgan — as respectively 'successful, 'good' and 'competent' teachers. Rice also described Richards as satisfactory in her probationary year. At the inquiry he praised McWhirter's teaching, and all opposing parties agreed that Austin and Chowles were marvellous. Was it then ILEA's view that Felton's and Green's classes were causing chaos?

On the contrary, the political rumours being circulated had been given credence by ILEA. An example of this can be seen in Bray's remarks to the staff in February 1975. The staff's united stances over dinner duties, the McColgan case and the London Allowance campaign had alienated them politically from the administration. Not only was the head not functioning as the Authority required, but, worse, he had been 'subverted' into the conspiracy.

County Hall has a fierce dislike of teacher militancy. One has only to point to the precipitous and harsh actions taken over the Houghton strikes, and the threats of fines and jail over the Tyndale strike of September 1975. With the NUT crushing of local branch autonomy, much militancy has been curbed. The only effective recourse now is for teachers to organise within their own schools, using them as a base for action. ILEA may have believed Tyndale

120

was the political cell it was rumoured to be, able to take unilateral political stances damaging to ILEA's image.

The Tyndale teachers will never know this for certain, as the ILEA's policy for dealing with their case was one of secrecy. Meetings were held behind closed doors both at Divisional Office and County Hall with Page, the managers, Hart and her staff, Chowles and Walker. The rest of the staff were excluded from all of them. These meetings discussed the future of the school, its possible reorganisation or closure, the health and tenure of its head, the teaching methods, the political and racial beliefs of its teachers. Inspections were discussed, along with press leaks, petitions and resolutions, 'spies', and allegations of racism.

All the staff ever knew of them were the distortions of rumour-mongering. This sort of closed government which Ellis attacked so eloquently at the inquiry cannot be conducted for the good of those excluded, or they would be informed and their opinions sought. The staff were given good reason to believe the authority were involved in a conspiracy against them.

Whatever the motives behind ILEA policy, the resulting chaos has cost them dearly in prestige and public opinion. The strike in September 1975 raised the affair to a national level, and the public interest in the inquiry opened up the inner workings of the authority, with all its scars and blemishes.

Chapter 11
July 24 – September 22 1975

The Inquiry files contain over 600 documents. 80 of these cover this period, of which five weeks were the summer holidays. The documents are largely concerned with the efforts of both staff and managers to secure some satisfactory guarantees and information about the inquiry, and ILEA's responses to those attempts. The extent of the correspondence illustrates the mistrust both parties felt about the ILEA package. But the authority had become a prisoner of its own formula and time-table, and, in trying to get things over quickly, managed to do the opposite.

The inquiry, as originally conceived, was to be conducted by five members of the Schools Sub-Committee. ILEA was to sit as judge and jury in its own case, since the same group would consider what action to take on the inquiry report. The panel later changed to four members and an independent chairman, and, later still, one member was to be a teacher from ILTA. This, understandably, did not meet with Tennant's approval. Much argument centred around who was to be the chairman (Tennant at one time suggested Lord Vic Feather); it was finally decided it should be a lawyer from the panel that ran ILEA's disciplinary tribunals. Both staff and managers feared a short ILEA-dominated inquiry would not unmask the

122

authority's role in the affair. The hurriedly erected edifice of inspection and inquiry was already beginning to show cracks.

The school's complement of full-time teachers had been reduced by one. Buckton had left, and Austin had become part-time, being responsible for remedial reading and development of the school's store of books. The standard of general stock and equipment had risen considerably. The managers were to claim, in the inquiry, that Ellis had been dilatory in spending money allocated to the school; but the staff had disposed of their allowance so enthusiastically that they had already overspent by September 1975.

Drawing on the experience of the previous year, and a staff stability which had never been achieved before, it was decided to develop the organisation into the following structure:

The children transferred from the Infants' were to be in two separate groups, with McColgan and Richards. The rest were to be in five 'vertical' groups, each not encompassing more than a two-year age span. Chowles, Haddow and McWhirter were to take the older children; Felton and Green the younger. During morning sessions each group was to work with its own teacher on basic skills. Each afternoon, a wide system of options was to be offered, co-ordinated by McWhirter. Ellis was timetabled to work in the options system. All classes were moved to the top floor; rooms on the middle floor were made specialist areas for art and music. The hall, now fitted with bookshelves and soft chairs, became a central reading area, and maintained its function as an area for social gatherings of staff and children.

Despite the abnormal conditions, this new departure showed every sign of working well. But it was only to last for three weeks.

It was all very well for managers and ILEA to talk of the future of the school. The teachers were afraid the inquiry would turn into a disciplinary tribunal against them, that the school's future was conceived by ILEA, as well as by certain managers, as something not requiring their presence. The inquiry was just another pressure, without any guarantees.

When term started in September the teachers were carrying on several lines of argument and negotiation, to secure an inquiry they could see as fair and impartial. These were: to negotiate with, and seek information from, Hinds; to negotiate through the inspectorate; to continue pressure for a DES inquiry; and to build support for their case among parents and other NUT members.

Correspondence with Hinds about ILEA proposals began on August 29th, and continued on September 3rd, 6th, 11th, and 15th. These letters stated the mounting opposition to ILEA's solution, and the lack of belief in its impartiality, while asking for a clear definition of the scope of the proceedings, and trying to elicit more general information — including, most vital of all, the availability of documents (the petition and Rice's report were of particular importance).

Whether Hinds was unwilling or unable to do this is not clear. His replies were not reassuring. The staff became more and more apprehensive, feeling a machine was in motion that no one could or would stop. The ruthless logic of the July 10th decision was being worked out, and they were subject to its laws. By September 11th, the heat was rising, and was reflected in the tone of the letter the teachers sent that day: 'We are now of the opinion that this unprecedented attack on a school and its staff has gone beyond our extreme toleration.' They talked of 'a witch hunt' and promised 'action against this decision'.

How could Hinds carry on believing the staff would accept his inquiry package? Tennant, also in communication about the inquiry, had sensed the danger. He asked Hinds what he would do if the staff refused to co-operate. Hinds said he would hope to persuade them. He then broke off negotiations, by second-class mail, on September 15th. In a later newspaper interview Tennant blamed Hinds for the teachers' strike.

It has often been stated that the Tyndale staff wanted to avoid inspection. This is untrue. It was this particular inquiry, the way it had been set up and was being organised, that they objected to. The inspection was not a normal one. Its purpose was to gather evidence, in the teachers' view an illegitimate use of a procedure ostensibly designed to help a school evaluate its work. A more passive group would have accepted it, for want of something better. The Tyndale teachers had never been known for their passivity, and had tolerated too much to start learning it now.

On August 27th Pape informed the school of the inspection dates. Ellis immediately asked him to speak to the staff, since most had serious reservations about the business. On September 10th Pape and Rice visited both schools. When the time came to speak to the Junior staff, Pape informed them that Rice had to leave as he had a prior appointment. At the inquiry, Rice said he left because Pape

124

told him to.

The staff said that the inquiry decision affected their deepest interests, but had been taken with no consultation and with no guarantees of fairness. Pape told them his inspection would not investigate the role of managers nor any political question, that he had no power to change its time or nature, and was dependent on instructions from superiors. He said it could not be assumed that Rice's report was on balance satisfactory (though Hinds had said it was). Pape's view was that the staff might need to go to the High Court to prove that contention about the Rice report.

The staff were also worried about retrospective criticisms of the school. They knew that complaints had been made by parents, but not dealt with by the authority. Now it appeared that Rice had been critical in his report. Would these complaints and criticisms influence the inspectors? Would they be brought up in the inquiry, even though ILEA had not acted at the time? Pape did not have the power to give any assurance that the staff's interests would be safeguarded. He had no influence over the inquiry, even though he was directing the evidence-gathering exercise. Pape's visit further convinced the staff that by participating in the inquiry they were following a very dangerous path.

On September 18th, Maths Inspector Peter Kaner made a pre-inspection visit. He admitted the inspectors were not anxious to come into the school. The staff put their case to him, and he tried to contact Birchenough. Failing to do so he finally got in touch with Pape. Later that day Pape telephoned. He was willing to have further discussions, but could not change the nature of the inspection. He had no intention of visiting the school to get involved in 'political' questions. He was willing to omit 'retrospective judgements' from consideration by the inspectors.

What did this mean? Whose judgements? What guarantees were there that these would also be omitted from the inquiry? If the school had done praiseworthy things in the past, would this also be omitted? Nothing was clear, because the inspection was being undertaken before anybody knew what the inquiry was going to consider, and how it was going to consider it. A general statement had been sent out by ILEA, and that was all. The confusion is illustrated by the fact that, when the inquiry opened in late October, and when it reconvened following another adjournment Chairman Robin Auld had to decide with ILEA and the various parties exactly what he was supposed to consider. If Auld was in comparative darkness at that advanced stage, one can imagine the impenetrable blackness in which staff and managers were lost in September.

On September 15th a letter from the DES told the staff that ILEA was to be allowed to undertake its own inquiry. The last hope for intervention by an outside body had disappeared.

At a general meeting of the NLTA on September 8th another resolution was passed in support of the Tyndale teachers. The association opposed any inspection before the inquiry. The teachers were willing to undergo inspection if, after a full inquiry, this was thought necessary for the future of the school.

The Support Campaign had been distributing information leaflets to parents. On September 17th a meeting was held to explain the situation to them. Only 8 parents came. The affair had by that time attained the length and complexity of a Russian novel, and was extremely difficult to make understandable without a welter of detail. The adverse press coverage had confused parents. To this must be added that natural indifference that the staff had been trying to combat during the past year. Many parents would come to see their own children's work, but to interest them in a general argument connected with the politics of education was another matter.

Tennant visited the school and discussed the inquiry and other matters with Ellis. The managers, he said, were perturbed about developments. He criticised Haddow's conduct in managers' meetings. The teacher-manager's past efforts to put the staff's point of view were summed up in one word — 'silly'. So much for democratically elected managers. He was no more complimentary about the leaders of ILEA — they were simply 'failed politicians'. Looking forward to the situation after the inquiry, he said that he would be happy if some of the managers ceased to be managers, provided the staff promised to 'behave' and Ellis manipulated Haddow off the managing body.

By September 19th the staff saw no way of deflecting by indirect means the threat of the ILEA solution. They had tried, argued and negotiated for long enough, without response. There was only one way left, even though it might mean further public pillorying and the disruption of what they had achieved. They felt that a stand had to be made, Ellis, Haddow, McColgan, McWhirter,

Richards, Green and Felton decided the inspection, the first stage of the inquiry, would be met by a withdrawal of labour, and that they would remain on strike until their demands for a fair proceeding were met.

This same day Briault at last contacted the school. He had been informed that the staff were having 'a little difficulty' with the inspection. When Ellis informed him of the proposed action, his coolness vanished. 'You're mad, you're all mad! What a way to start the inquiry!' But the teachers had not started the inquiry; ILEA, of which Briault was the chief official, had. He abruptly ordered Ellis to bring the staff to County Hall after school, and replaced the receiver.

The decision had been taken. Parents and ILEA officials, including Pape and Briault, were informed by letter that the school would be closed the following Monday.

On September 20th, Walker wrote again to Boyson. The letter contained a long attack on Ellis and those who supported him; Walker made it clear she considered them a danger to society, part of a group of teachers who were making state education a shambles. 'I am aware of the fact that it will be extremely difficult to prove the political motivation of Mr Ellis and his staff', she wrote, with reference to the coming inquiry. 'Personally, I feel that if the right questions were put in the inquiry it would not be impossible to trap Ellis and company into admitting their political aims, but it would require clever tactics. Meanwhile I have been advised by Mr Tennant, the chairman of the managers, that I should renew my membership of the NUT . . . as they would be bound to give me legal protection.'

In a curious way, the wheel had come full circle.

Chapter 12
The National Union of Teachers

The NUT is the largest and most important teachers' union in Britain. Because of its size and income it offers many services of value to teachers. However there are occasions, increasingly frequent during the last few years, on which it has discriminated between members in the support it offers. There are two principal reasons for such discrimination; the structure of the union, and the political attitude of the leadership.

The union has about 600 constituent or local associations, grouped and organised to be coterminous with LEA areas. The associations elect delegates to annual conference, the policy making body, and, organised into electoral districts, individual members elect the executive by ballot. This structure differs from most unions in that an overwhelming majority of the honorary offices are held by members representing a fraction of the membership. Head teachers make up about 8% of full-time teachers in the country, yet in the NUT they hold a majority of Executive seats, and at local levels a similar pattern exists. Since one of the principal tasks of a head is to act as a personnel manager for the LEA, even the most benevolent has a perpetual conflict of interests when holding union office.

Many of these heads come from primary schools outside the

conurbations and, in addition to office in the union, hold a disproportionate number of delegate seats at the annual conference. This imbalance is historical, since heads have always had access to facilities essential for trade union branch officers, whereas class teachers often cannot even make or receive phone calls during working hours. It requires courage to stand or vote against your head in union elections, when he or she controls your working conditions and, to a large extent, your career prospects.

In London there are eleven local associations, which make up the Inner London Teachers' Association (ILTA), the negotiating body with the employer, ILEA. The North London Teachers' Association (NLTA), which serves Islington has had the reputation of being one of the most militant branches. With other London associations, it was instrumental in pushing the union nationally towards the use of industrial action in the salaries struggle. The NLTA was in the front in struggles to improve teachers' conditions, and has campaigned vigorously on size of classes and the extension of democracy within schools.

Because of its activities and policies, the NLTA has been less than popular with both the ILEA and the union hierarchy. This suspicion was increased in the late 1960s and early 1970s, because many of the most active members had sympathies with the Rank and File organisation, set up in 1968 as a 'ginger group' of NUT members. Rank and File came into existence because of growing dissatisfaction with the lack of vigour shown by the NUT in defending teachers' interests.

The ILEA and NUT have always been ambivalent towards Rank and File. Publicly the ILEA ignores its existence. The NUT cannot, but claims it is a tiny minority of unrepresentative individuals. Privately both authority and union officials devote much time and effort attempting to curb its influence. Since 1968 two presidents of the NLTA have been subjected to ILEA disciplinary procedures, in which their views and activities as Rank and File members were brought up against them. In one of these cases the union provided an official as 'prosecutor' in the proceedings. The official antagonism against Rank and File is such that teachers who are merely personal friends of members can find their careers running into difficulties.

Only one of the Tyndale staff, McColgan, was a member of Rank and File. Her arrival at the school in April 1974 was an important factor in determining the attitude of the authority and the NUT. The principle of guilt by association is firmly established in North London, as was shown by inferences behind some of the questioning of witnesses at the inquiry.

The job of any union is to defend and protect its members. When trouble began in 1974 they moved, through the proper channels, to get union help. Knowing an attack on the head and staff was planned for a parents' meeting in July 1974, they consulted Horace Perrin, London Regional Official of the NUT. Perrin's advice was that the head would have to attend, but the other teachers should not. In spite of a request that a union observer attend no one was sent, and, as forecast, an attack on the school was made.

Throughout July and the summer holiday of 1974, Haddow sent to the union documented evidence of political interference with the school. At the end of August Ellis placed in the hands of the union a full account of the events of the previous term. Perrin wrote back to Ellis in the middle of September, hoping that life would become more tolerable during the coming year. Life, however, was not more tolerable, since many problems remained unresolved. A month later the staff asked the NLTA officers for advice and support. A letter expressing the unanimous support of the NLTA committee was sent to the school. When a crisis point was again reached in May 1975, the school's problems were laid before the general meetings of the NLTA in June, July and September.

Several Tyndale managers were interested in NLTA meetings, and seemed to have inside information about what took place there. When, in June 1975, the association backed the staff by asking other schools not to accept transfers from Tyndale, Hoodless had a copy of the resolution the next day, and immediately sent it to Hinds. Burnett told the inquiry this resolution had roused her to anger, and as a result she began collecting signatures for the petition her Labour Party friends had produced. A third manager, Fairweather, told some Tyndale teachers that the July meeting of the NLTA had not been properly constituted. Since she was not a teacher or NUT member, she was not aware the meeting she complained of was the regular monthly meeting, of which due notice had been given.

All the resolutions of support for Tyndale put during summer 1975 received overwhelming backing from the NLTA. The association took a strong line from the beginning of the debates in the general meeting, and in June 1975 decided the following:

1   The NLTA condemns the vicious campaign over the last thirteen months against the staff of William Tyndale school.

2   The falling roll resulting from this campaign has serious implications for the staff. We therefore call upon NLTA members in neighbouring schools to oppose admission to their schools of children from William Tyndale Junior and Infant Schools.

3   We call upon the NUT legal department to take action to defend the teachers under attack.'

The Tyndale teachers felt reassured by this support when they went to discuss the situation with Hinds and the school managers at County Hall on July 2nd. They were accompanied by NLTA Secretary Smith, and Perrin.

Prior to this, the staff had been trying to see Perrin for six weeks, but though the school is only a couple of miles from NUT headquarters, Perrin produced a succession of reasons as to why a meeting was impossible. At one time he was under the weather, at another his failing eyesight meant he could not read a photocopied document, and a meeting had to be postponed until he received a copy he found more legible. At other times appointments were made and cancelled at the last moment, because of other more urgent business. Two days before the Hinds meeting Perrin turned up at the school, but the only advice he could give was: 'Play it cool and leave the talking to one or two people.'

On the day of the meeting Smith, who is also a teacher representative on ILEA, paid a surprise visit to the school. He showed the staff an agenda paper for the joint steering committee of the London Borough of Islington and ILEA. The staff knew nothing of the committee, but could see the school was listed for discussion a week or so later. Smith told them they were being used in a battle between ILEA and Islington.

The meeting started badly when Hinds intimated the teachers could not put their case because there was a possibility of a complaint being laid against them for excluding the managers. Together with Perrin and Smith, they withdrew to consider the position and, largely as a result of NUT advice, agreed to return to the meeting. It became clear later that this was a mistake, and they should have insisted on a meeting where they would be allowed to present their point of view.

When the managers proposed that the staff join in a call to the

DES for a general inspection, Hinds was obviously not in favour of the proposal. It was Perrin who claimed, contrary to Hinds' assertion, that a DES inspection could be organised with great speed.

Smith had taken little part in the discussions, and left early. The next day he wrote to Hinds:

'Dear Harvey,

May I say that I was filled with admiration for the way in which you chaired the meeting. Both sides seemed to me to be well stocked with difficult people who were not in the least interested in your efforts to obtain reconciliation.'

Yet the very reason why Smith was present at the meeting was at the request of the teachers, in an attempt to resolve their problems.

Five days later the details of the County Hall meeting were reported to the NLTA, which reaffirmed its support for excluding the managers, and for demands for an investigation into the managers' actions. Smith did not repeat his compliments to Hinds, and did nothing to oppose the motion.

By September the situation had grown more complicated. Perrin had, at the teachers' request, applied to ILEA for certain documents, and having been refused decided there was nothing more he could do. The staff knew the inspectors would not investigate the matters they had been raising throughout the previous year. They decided they must insist on the principle that there must be an inquiry before any inspection took place, and that the precise nature of the inquiry must be specified before they could agree to take part. In this they had the support of the NLTA, which on September 8th passed a resolution incorporating this principle.

However the ILTA officers met and, without consulting the Tyndale staff, decided they should cooperate with the inspection, and leave the matter of attendance at any inquiry in abeyance. ILTA secretary Robert Richardson got in touch with ILEA to inform them of the NLTA decision. A memo from Birchenough to Briault, dated September 11th 1975, read: 'I understand informally from ILTA officials that a resolution was passed by NLTA on Monday 8th September calling on ILTA to demand that no inspection should precede the necessary investigation into the actions of the managers. (This is not verbatim but the general sense of the motion.) Mr Richardson is likely to approach the Leader and Mr Hinds shortly,

132

probably to suggest a postponement of the inspection and inquiry to allow for attempts to settle the problem by other means during this term.'

No one told the staff of any approach by Richardson, and no documents were produced to the inquiry to show he had made representations on this question. It appears from Birchenough's memo that he was anxious to point to ways in which matters might be smoothed over, but it seems NUT officials were not prepared to take any positive and helpful steps. There could hardly be a greater condemnation of the NUT, since it was certainly in the teachers' interest to avoid a confrontation, and ILEA were obviously looking to the NUT for help in solving their problems.

On September 15th a special meeting of the NLTA to discuss Tyndale was requisitioned. This was to be held on September 24th. Also on the evening of the 15th the General Purposes Committee of the NLTA met, and decided that at the special meeting they would move a motion effectively rescinding the policy decided at the general meeting on September 8th. The crucial principle which was association policy was that an inquiry should precede an inspection. The committee stated in their motion that they still supported the staff but that they should cooperate with the inspection and that action had already been taken on the other policies decided upon by the general meeting. This was untrue, and shown to be so when the Birchenough memo was revealed. Other evidence given to the inquiry showed that the only element of NLTA policy that had been taken up by the ILTA was the demand for teacher representation on the inquiry.

Smith did not inform the staff of this proposal to reverse policy, and they still expected that on September 16th the NLTA resolution would go before the ILTA Council for ratification.

This did not happen. At the Council Richardson brought up the Tyndale case in the officers' report which, for procedural reasons, is not open to challenge. He recommended that the Tyndale teachers cooperate with the inspection. Decisions were being taken and recommendations made without those concerned being consulted.

Once the staff decided to take action to defend their interests, the union moved rapidly *against* the teachers. There was no lack of communication between teachers and union at that point. Since they took this decision independently of the union, the Union's officers had no knowledge of a possible strike.

During the afternoon of that day Briault had been told over the phone by Ellis that the staff were to strike on the following Monday; his response had been to tell Ellis to make them come to County Hall at 4 pm. This they did not do, although some went with a letter to inform Briault that they would be striking from the 22nd. Briault had gone home by the time they arrived, presumably taking for granted that the teachers had gone on strike. Shortly after 5 pm the NUT phoned the school, to transmit a message from the Executive that the staff must not take strike action. Since no teacher had been in touch with the union after the strike decision was taken, it must be assumed that the union was acting on information from Briault. It was remarkable that the union could enter into transactions with the employer without ever consulting those at risk, and yet, at the employer's behest, immediately re-establish communication. General Secretary Fred Jarvis, who had not seen fit to intervene when the teachers had been under attack from the press, over the next few days sent letters to each member, threatening disciplinary action.

The day after the strike began a meeting was held at County Hall. Bramall and Hinds were present, with Briault and Burgess. The union was represented by Richardson and Perrin. The minute of that meeting shows that they were worried that the NLTA, which was to hold its special meeting the next day, would support the strike. They agreed that the 'facts' must be put before the special meeting, and this responsibility was accepted by the union. A selective collection of letters was prepared and duplicated during the next twenty-four hours, for distribution to those who were to attend the special MLTA meeting. Smith prepared overnight a lengthy document to justify the reversal of policy by the NLTA committee. The effect of this material was to create the impression that there were no issues of importance other than the proposed inspection which, it was obliquely suggested, would be bound to be favourable to the teachers. No mention was made of the activities of the managers, or of the unprecedented barrage of false political allegations the press had carried.

When the special meeting opened the atmosphere was tense. Normally about one hundred members attended meetings but, on this occasion, almost two hundred were present. Many of these had never been seen at union meetings, and some teachers arrived in groups led into the hall by their head teacher.

Those present at the earlier meetings on Tyndale knew the

fundamental issue was simple. The ILEA proposal for an inspection was, in the eyes of the Tyndale teachers and all those who supported them, an attempt to sidestep the investigation of the political attacks on the school. The NLTA had recognised this two weeks earlier, when it decided that an inquiry into these matters must precede any inspection. In opposing any other arrangement the Tyndale staff were acting consistently, and in accordance with NLTA policy. ILEA had ignored the political campaign in the press, and its arrangements for inspection had led many of the public to believe there was substance in the allegations of political indoctrination and the fomenting of 'revolutionary' activities.

Ellis and Haddow proposed and seconded the motion. They reported the latest developments, and moved that the association stand by its policy of support for the Tyndale staff. The President called four speakers to support the motion, and four to oppose.

The first to speak against was Smith. His argument was interesting. Briault had threatened the staff with prosecution for obstructing an inspection. Smith argued that since legal sanctions had been proposed against the teachers they could not be supported by the union.

He was followed by a member of the association committee, who argued that since it had been stated by Hinds that Rice's secret report on the school was favourable, by agreeing to the inspection the school would receive confirmation of this favourable report. The would receive conclusive confirmation of this favourable report. The essence of this speech was that ILEA could be trusted implicitly to look after the interests of its teachers. No one knew until much later that for more than a year the ILEA had been collecting complaints against the teachers, and filing them at County Hall.

Two others spoke against the motion. Margaret Maden, head of Islington Green Comprehensive, had come to the area a year before, but up to September 1975 had attended few union meetings. She had built up a powerful public image as a speaker on education, and was often to be seen on television. She spoke with passion about teacher accountability, and claimed the Tyndale staff were shirking their responsibilities to the public. Nothing was said about the accountability of school managers and governors. Maden had on her board of governors two people whose activities have already been documented: Page and Mabey.

The last speaker to oppose was Chris King who had, up to that time, supported association policy on Tyndale. King was known to be a 'militant' and a Rank and File supporter, and his speech surprised many. He put forward an argument about teacher accountability and, like the other opposition speakers, showed little concern about the political attacks on the school which, by this time, had been extended to political attacks on the NLTA. Shortly after this meeting King became a Labour borough councillor. Along with Maden, he has not been seen at NLTA meetings since.

Those speaking for the motion in addition to Ellis and Haddow were the immediate past president of the association Ann Yaffe, and Jeff Hurford, later secretary of the William Tyndale Support Campaign. Yaffe stated that it was not true, as had been claimed, that the committee had been unanimously in favour of a policy reversal. Hurford pointed out that the circumstances which had led the association to back the Tyndale staff had not changed, and that the teachers' resistance to ILEA's arrangements was a logical consequence of association policy over the previous three months.

Feelings ran high: there were angry exchanges between individuals and groups. Those who had attended the earlier meetings were angry that policy was being overturned by people who had rarely been seen at meetings and who they believed correctly, they would never see again. The motion of support was lost, and the amendment drafted by Smith, which called on the teachers to accept an inspection before an inquiry, was carried by 110 to 77. Whilst the amendment said the association supported the staff on all points other than the central issue, it was immediately interpreted by ILEA as a withdrawal of backing for Tyndale. Whilst there *was* no official union support for the teachers, the level of unofficial backing from individuals and schools increased greatly, and financial and moral support came not only from London but from all over the country.

The ILEA's interest in the affairs of the NLTA was demonstrated by Hinds' evidence to the inquiry, when he said: 'The activities of the NLTA are, from time to time, a matter of discussion within this building [County Hall]'. Page obviously took an interest in the workings of the NLTA and the composition of its committees. In her evidence she said she had friendly contacts with Smith, from whom she must have learnt that he and treasurer Ron Lendon were in no way militants, and that the current association committee was made up of like-minded people. Despite this knowledge, she was so concerned about the NLTA that she wrote to Hinds early in 1975, 136 saying it was time 'the NLTA nettle was grasped', and suggesting that this should be done by the ILEA rather than members of the public. Hinds said he thought she was referring to 'extreme left-wing officers at a certain period' and that she had in mind 'countering their activities'. Page claimed the ILEA had a long-standing fear of the NLTA, and had been afraid of 'a negative reaction' to anything that might be done about Tyndale. Some sections of the press had made direct attacks on the NLTA, and some of the inquiry witnesses tried to hint at political misdeeds by union members in North London. Counsel for Chowles, instructed by the NUT legal department, frequently demanded to know from witnesses whether they had any connection with Rank and File. At one point in the inquiry Auld intervened sharply, to ask whether it was being suggested that any teacher who supported Rank and File was thereby acting improperly as a teacher. No clear answer was given.

Another significant aspect of the NUT position at the Inquiry was the evidence given by Lendon, the NLTA treasurer. It was he who had advised Ellis to exclude managers in May 1975, and who had, at the beginning of September 1975, made a stirring speech in support of the staff, following it up by a personal note to the teachers, urging them to 'keep on fighting'. NUT counsel said early in the inquiry that it was on the basis of Lendon's advice that Chowles had signed the letter excluding the managers. The ILEA barrister also stated that this exclusion was based on union advice.

Jarvis issued a statement to the press denying that any such advice had been given. The result was that Lendon had to attend the inquiry, and was placed in a highly embarrassing position. In his evidence he had to claim that any advice he gave was given to Ellis as a fellow head, and not as a union officer. Auld asked: 'Why, then, out of all the London headteachers, should Ellis turn to you for advice?' Lendon had to admit it was because he was an officer of the union. A telling illustration of the NUT's attitude is a remark reported in *The Times Educational Supplement*. Senior NUT solicitor Kenneth Wormald was quoted as saying that his union was on the side of the 'goodies' in the inquiry. Even before the inquiry opened Max Morris, former NUT President, had gone on television to attack Ellis and his colleagues. At no time did any of the union leadership suggest judgement should be suspended until the facts had been investigated.

The leadership reaction to resolutions from local associations is equally enlightening. The resolutions of support for the school from NLTA were, so far as is known, never discussed at executive level, and obviously had no more value, in terms of official support at national level, than the paper they were written upon. Yet great importance was attached to the negotiations between ILEA and the ILTA officers, which effectively achieved a resolution which withdrew official local support from Ellis and his colleagues. Shortly after the Tyndale case the conference, at the instance of the Executive, changed the rules, to ensure they could instantly suspend, and discipline any teacher who, in the view of union officers, brought the union into disrepute.

The most important aspect of this new rule is that it will effectively prevent teachers from putting their case to their local associations if they are named under the rule by the appropriate officers of the union. Not only does it deprive the teacher of the opportunity to seek the support of fellow members; but if they seek to challenge the application of the rule, they are not allowed the services of a barrister or solicitor to defend themselves.

The Tyndale staff are not the only teachers to have come into conflict with the union, but their case is one of the few in which the nature of this conflict can be discerned. The union is directed largely by people who, as head teachers, see themselves as part of the management structure. The Tyndale teachers' action was a threat to that structure.

Chapter 13
September 22 – October 27 1975

The strike projected the school into national prominence. The teachers' faces became well-known, their opinions and news of their future actions eagerly sought by journalists; they were interviewed on radio, appeared on television, and spoke at meetings. Much of the publicity was unpleasant and distressing. They received the usual quota of obscene and abusive letters. In the middle of the furore, they patiently sought what they had always asked for — a fair and impartial inquiry. How far public exposure of their case helped achieve their aims is open to speculation, but in the end the inquiry did take a form, however imperfect, that met many of their objections.

On September 22nd they issued a press release, mounted a picket outside the school, and held a press conference. The release stated why they were going on strike, and their intention to remain until their demands were met. At the conference, they gave details of their case. The managers had been making the running in the press for too long, and the ILEA had done nothing to defend Tyndale from attack.

The decision to picket proved controversial. Many, including inspectors and managers, thought it disgraceful that children should see teachers undertaking what is normal in many industrial actions. Here we have the usual double standards in force; for teachers are no different from other workers with a deep grievance. Are they expected to set an example of mild obedience, even when they believe the orders are wrong?

No attempt was made to prevent any child from entering the school. The only obstructions were caused by hordes of eager reporters and photographers. Though the local police brought a dog along on one occasion, they expressed their satisfaction over the way in which the picket had been conducted. The pickets, actively supported by local teachers, continued throughout the strike.

Because of the allegations that had been made in the past, and were still being made the staff gave as many press interviews as possible, since their side of the story was still not emerging from reports.

When Ellis appeared on television with Tennant and Bramall, it became clear, during the discussion, that ILEA had acted precipitately in undertaking the inspection before the full facts about the inquiry had been made known. Bramall proved to be at variance with his own Press Office about the identity of the inquiry chairman, although it was later made known this would be Robin Auld, QC.

On September 23rd the staff received a letter from Briault instructing them to return to work. They were threatened with Section 77 of the Education Act, which prescribes fines and imprisonment for any teacher obstructing an inspection. In a radio interview, Ellis invited Briault to proceed with the sanction if he thought he had a case: this offer was never taken up. The letter only served to exacerbate a difficult situation. The NUT executive immediately notified ILEA that they did not support the Tyndale teachers' strike and later instructed their members to return to work in equally peremptory terms.

On the afternoon of September 23rd, the teachers went to meet Briault at County Hall. He attempted to persuade them to return to school, to be inspected. He accused Ellis of leading his staff astray by getting them to strike. This was hotly disputed by the other teachers, since the decision had been a joint one. What Briault said about the Inquiry only reinforced the teachers' fears — the petition and the Rice report would only be considered by the inquiry if ILEA thought fit. This was not to be so, because of the 'discovery'   140 of documents; but the staff could not know this would happen, and could only assume Briault knew what he was talking about. Neither party would budge, so the position remained unchanged.

Shortly afterwards on the same day, a conference was held between ILEA leaders and representatives of the London ILTA. The teachers had seen Richardson deep in conversation with Bramall's personal assistant as they, without union aid, were going to meet Briault.

Briault reported on his meeting with the teachers. He had apparently changed his mind about who was 'leading' the strike, and opted for the usual ILEA conspiracy theory that the staff were being led astray by one or two 'extremists'. He could not understand the staff's demands, although these were quite simple. This, in fact, illustrates how those who deal with teachers have no idea of common trade union practices. By their strike the teachers had placed themselves in danger of suspension and disciplinary action. But ILEA were caught on their own formula; to suspend would be to prejudice the inquiry. Their aim therefore was to induce the staff to return to school so the inspection/inquiry machine, now spluttering ominously, could roll forward again. The ILEA and the NUT therefore decided the 'facts' should be put before the NLTA when it met on September 24th, to consider its reaction to the Tyndale situation.

Two days after the strike began the Junior School was open again, with Rice in charge and the inspectors as teachers. Chowles and Arnold were still at work. Austin had not joined the strike, but refused to work with anybody except his usual colleagues, and therefore resigned. Although an ILEA official stated to the press that the inspectors were, as teachers, 'at the top of the tree', it became evident they were having difficulties in coping.

Ellis and Haddow now made a managers' visit to their own school, to establish that they were still members of the managing body. They should have been received by acting head Rice, but it seemed he was otherwise engaged, and they saw Pape instead. He refused them entry to the classrooms, on the basis of the staff's letter of exclusion of June 23rd. They did, however, make a report to Tennant about the difficulties the inspectors were having, simply to demonstrate how easy it was to find fault with a school by picking up and retailing scraps of gossip.

That evening, at a bitter, turbulent meeting, the NLTA refused support for the strike, and pressed the teachers to return to work. It still believed, however, that their original grievances were well-founded, and was to make a submission to the inquiry on their behalf.

This setback did not deflect the teachers. They undertook an extensive programme of visits to other schools and NUT local associations which passed motions of support and sent petitions to ILEA. The Support Campaign continued its activities. Information sheets were sent to every school in London. Money for the Tyndale Defence Fund poured in from sympathisers.

The ILEA Schools Sub-Committee had set up the inquiry. It was the only body that could change the nature of the ILEA package or offer negotiation in the conflict. It was due to meet on September 25th. It cancelled the meeting 'for lack of business'.

Later that week Briault again instructed the staff to return to work. He was, at the same time, conducting an acrimonious correspondence with Ellis about the latter's alleged breach of contract in closing the school without permission. After Ellis's second reply, Briault retired from the fray; ILEA never raised this 'charge' in the inquiry, nor did they present Briault as a witness.

A number of parents were keeping children away from the school as a gesture of support for the teachers. As their children were not at school, they were risking legal penalties as well as losing time from work to mind the children. The staff therefore decided to open, on September 29th, a 'strike' school for the duration of the dispute. A local church hall was rented. Parents were informed that this service was available, and a number took advantage of it.

It has often been stated, by those who should have known better (including Cunningham to the House of Commons), that the teachers 'encouraged' children away from Tyndale. This, besides being a falsehood, reveals a dishonesty of attitude. Both Cunningham and the managers professed themselves supporters of parents' rights, yet disapproved of the strike school when the parents exercised their rights to send their children there. Some managers even intimated that attempts would be made to get the new school closed. Yet in July Mabey, in his capacity as an Islington councillor, had offered parents aid in transferring children *from* Tyndale. But at that time the permanent staff were there; now they were outside. The view the managers and their supporters took of the strike school remains a prime example of 'double-think' in the Tyndale affair. The strike school duly opened at Gaskin Street Chapel, two hundred yards from the ILEA establishment, which continued to be picketed by staff and their supporters.

Gaskin Street School was run on voluntary contributions of materials, money and time from parents. Many showed great courage in sending their children there; fear of authority could have easily dissuaded them. One parent was approached by two people from the South Islington Labour Party, in an attempt to induce her to withdraw her children from the school. She refused. Gaskin Street continued until the teachers decided to co-operate with the inquiry. It was finally closed on October 14th. Its roll was never less than twenty-three, and never more than twenty-eight. Within the limitations of the building and the materials to hand, the staff provided a service for children who would not otherwise have gone to school.

Tennant now wished to meet some of the teachers to discuss the managers, meeting, which was due to consider the ILEA's proposals for future staffing of the school. On the 27th, Ellis, Haddow and McWhirter agreed to meet him. He believed certain teachers should be removed from the school, but did not specify which. Earlier that week a journalist had told the staff that managers he had interviewed had objected to Haddow and McColgan, but not on educational grounds. Tennant did not anticipate a return to work by the teachers, and said they would be opposed if they tried it.

The following day, the teachers met Larry Grant for the first time. A former NCCL lawyer, now at the University of Kent, he came in contact with the teachers through Dick North, a member of the NUT Executive, who supported them. Since they were in conflict with the union, Grant agreed to act for them if they were to decide to co-operate with the inquiry. He was later to secure the services of barrister Stephen Sedley.

The managers' meeting of September 29th must have been the first such gathering to be picketed, and held with a police guard. Tennant refused to allow a parent and some members of the Support Campaign to attend as observers. After about an hour the meeting adjourned, and a private gathering without teachers, and without Divisional Officer Price, who was acting as clerk, took place. When the official meeting re-convened the managers made a formal complaint against the striking teachers.

This procedure was incorrect. The rules make it clear that

discussion about a complaint should be recorded by the clerk, not carried on in secret. But Tennant had not finished yet. Complaints are supposed to be confidential; this too is laid down in the rulebook. Yet Tennant immediately leaked the news to a reporter with whom he had a prior arrangement. The staff complained to Hinds and Briault about Tennant's conduct at this meeting.

The managers' complaint placed ILEA in more difficulty. Birchenough had indicated strong action should be taken against the teachers. But how could the ILEA convene a disciplinary tribunal without destroying their inquiry? If they held their inquiry, no disciplinary action could be taken until it reported. The procedure that had kept others in a strait-jacket was now starting to tie ILEA in knots. They took no action on the complaint, hoping the teachers would return to work to be inspected.

All the teachers' communications with ILEA were now undertaken by Grant. He had asked for numerous documents which they would require for their case. This was simply an expansion of their demands of September 22nd. When they received most of the papers, they felt participation in the inquiry might be possible. It was, despite all their objections, the only procedure for bringing into the open the machinations that had led to the conflict. With adequate information, which they at last appeared to be getting, they had a chance of presenting a case. They therefore took the decision to 'buy' the ILEA package — which would mean returning to school.

On October 6th a further managers' meeting was held. The school had been staffed since September 29th, when the inspectors left, by senior head teachers and peripatetics. The managers wished this to continue, but some were aware the permanent staff might be contemplating a return. Mabey put a motion that they should not be allowed to do so until after the inquiry, which he now did not think 'paramount' anyway. All he succeeded in doing was splitting the managing body.

George Martindale, Chairman of the Islington Trades Council, objected to what he saw as a 'lock-out'. A heated discussion ensued, and the motion was passed, with more abstentions than votes. Hart voted in favour of keeping her fellow NUT members out of their school. She and Jay were later to express the view at County Hall that Ellis and company should be excluded. Infant parents canvassed yet another petition, asking for this exclusion.

144

Ellis protested about Tennant's release of confidential information to the press. Hoodless persuaded the managers to support Tennant's action in a formal motion, and later suggested more information be given to the press to force some action out of Hinds. It appeared that the managers were making up the rules as they went along, and that ILEA had lost control not only of a teaching staff but also of a managing body.

Although only Chowles and Arnold had been present in the school, Pape produced a report on October 7th, collated from notes made by individual inspectors. Birchenough's comment was that these were 'partially factual and partially subjective'. Pape made the point, at the beginning of the report, that the school could not be fully inspected in the absence of staff. He then produced 4,000 words to describe this non-inspection. The second inspection report, produced on the period when the teachers were back in the school, was only slightly longer. The October 7th report was savagely critical, in contrast to that which Infant Inspector Goddard gave to the Infants. It appeared that the best and worst schools in London were in the same building.

Welch's memorandum is an example of the kind of material Pape worked from. Welch himself calls it a 'jeremiad'. It is written in highly-coloured language, and finds nothing to commend. It attacks the Steel Band, the children's behaviour, their attainment, and above all the staff, whom he had never met. But where are the facts? He finds nine year olds who cannot use a ruler or spell very well; but any London school has these, and surely he knew it. Where are the comparisons with the rest of the school, or with other schools? Where are the attainment tests?

The lack of factual evidence in the inspection reports is noticeable; they often tell more of the inspectors' attitudes than of the state of Tyndale. Welch begins his poem in purple with a reference to the school's name, which he says derives from the famous Protestant martyr, but which, in fact, refers to an obscure local landowner. Welch's attack may be an extreme example; other reports are only slightly more temperate.

On October 8th Pape, realising the teachers might return, told Briault and Birchenough the school would need at least two weeks to get back to anything like normality. Yet when they returned, Pape was there to greet them with the news that the inspection would re-commence immediately.

But the staff were not to have an easy road back. The managers had been led to believe that the ILEA would not stand idly by while the teachers returned. When it appeared on October 15th that a return was imminent, Mabey tried to get an injunction to prevent it. Tennant, Hoodless and Gittings met, and planned the distribution of the first inspection report, which ILEA had forgotten to mark 'confidential', to the press. This was a deliberate and meticulously planned action; it involved a careful list of newspapers, messengers, and the most appropriate methods of transport to use, all drawn up by Hoodless. As a tactic to prevent the teachers returning, it was a failure. But it did provoke the kind of reaction that ensured the return took place in the most distressing circumstances possible. The press eagerly abstracted the criticisms in the report, and blazed them across the front pages. The staff were crucified.

October 16th was, without a doubt, the most harrowing day in the Tyndale affair. The teachers were escorted by the police through a crowd of hostile parents, a flock of reporters, and a battery of cameras. They wished to co-operate with the inspection, but feared for their physical safety and that of the children. Parents came in and dragged their children out when they saw the permanent staff were back. The crowd outside the gate swelled, and was assiduously courted by the journalists for critical comments.

The teachers were in; the managers redoubled their efforts to get them out again. On October 17th a delegation, which included Hoodless and Tennant, met top ILEA representatives, including Bramall, Briault and Hinds, at County Hall. The managers wanted the teachers suspended, and even offered their own suspension in exchange. But managers cannot be suspended. They tried to invoke their own official complaint and the alleged breach of Section 77 — all to no avail. The inspection/inquiry fiasco would have reached the heights of absurdity had ILEA suspended the staff because they wanted to return to work, when ILEA orders had been that the staff should do precisely this. The managers were thwarted, and the inspection continued.

In this ILEA exercise, which lasted from October 16th until October 23rd, there were elements not out of place in the Theatre of the Absurd. For the inspection to retain any validity, it was necessary for Pape to suppress his own opinions, and act as though he was assessing a school in normal circumstances. He began on October 16th as though the teachers had not been away for nearly 146 four weeks, although it was obvious the school they had returned to was totally changed. The children had been put in different classes, furniture had been rearranged, the reading and social areas dismantled, equipment and books lost. Only about fifty children attended, and some teachers had classes of only three. They were nevertheless to undergo with due solemnity an 'inspection' of their work, with the evidence provided being used to attack them in the inquiry.

Events, however, conspired against the pretence, and the farcical nature of the proceedings kept breaking through. The inspectors arrived timidly, obviously conditioned to find a band of wild revolutionaries, and being surprised at the politeness and calmness of their reception. One inspector got so confused she started questioning one of her colleagues, under the impression that this person was a teacher, and was nonplussed to receive uninformative answers. Ellis and Pape spent hours in the head's room, engaged in Pinteresque verbal sparring bouts, each conscious that anything said might be 'taken down' and used in evidence in the inquiry.

When not thus engaged, Pape moved in stately manner about the corridors, punctuating his progress with the occasional sortie into a classroom. He was particularly unlucky with Haddow, who always seemed to be on the point of leaving his class for P.E., swimming or games, every time the inspector came to see him. 'Ah, foiled again, Mr. Haddow,' said Pape on the third occasion. Haddow was also taken to task by Ryder, Inspector for Learning Resources, because he had old-fashioned and irrelevant reading material in his room. Before the strike the staff had cleared out all this material, and placed it in boxes for disposal: the temporary staff had redistributed it among the classes. In McColgan's class the greatest farce of all was enacted. She taught, and was inspected, while a carpenter hammered away at a broken window-frame laid out on the floor of her room. How it was possible to get any true picture of the school is not clear.

Pape, in his second report, asserted that the school, as it really was, had not been inspected, and asserted it at great length, with damaging criticisms of the staff who had been on strike. All the returning teachers knew that such a report would be made, and that it would be used against them in the inquiry. They were under considerable mental stress, and, in normal circumstances, some of

147

them might well have sought medical advice instead of attending school. Richards was taken seriously ill during the inspection, but attended when she was able. What had been called 'the delicate professional relationship' between staff and inspectors was effectively destroyed by the second inspection, despite the surface politeness which led Pape to say that the staff had behaved 'professionally'.

The second inspection report was produced to all parties shortly before the inquiry, and, later, the memoranda on which both reports were based were put in evidence. Both inspection reports were hedged about with reservations.

The inspections were supposed to be fact-finding exercises for the inquiry. One of the most remarkable things is the facts they did not find, and the dubious nature of those they did. The only attempt to test the children's attainment was carried out by Geddes during the second inspection. In the main report, Pape refers to this as follows: 'The wide variation in facility with language is borne out in the diagnostic testing, which was done during the visit.' The first sentence of Geddes memorandum concerning this testing reads: 'This is not intended for use as a diagnostic test.'

The Geddes 'test' did not conform to the standards set by educational researchers. It bore no indication of its origin, nor stated for whom it was designed or the age range to which it was applicable. No information on standardised results was provided or ever made available to the inquiry, nor was it made clear how this test came into existence. The 'test' report abounded in arithmetical errors; as a result the percentages calculated were in error by as much as 15%. A further error was created by assuming two thirds of the children not tested (half the school was absent at the time of the second inspection) were of low attainment. The test purported to show that only 28% of the children were competent readers. The lowest scores were achieved by those just arrived from the Infants', which had just received the accolades of the inspectorate.

A large amount of information available was never presented by the inspectors to the inquiry. Records of reading tests conducted in both Infant and Junior Schools were in existence. These were never sought by the inspectors. Rice, for example, knew of the Junior reading records because he had been shown them. Did he not communicate his knowledge to Pape? If he did, why did Pape not procure copies for the inquiry? Pape's explanation was that it was up to the staff to tell him of such information. But ILEA had never before taken the view that staff should be carefully consulted before information was sought about their work; why should they start now? The vast majority of the reading records were already in ILEA's possession, as part of the documentation provided by both schools for transfer procedures, both from Infant to Junior School and from Junior to Secondary. Pape, as an ILEA inspector of long standing, must have known this, and he was in charge of ILEA's evidence-gathering mssion. This he did not do, although such factual evidence is of more value, where serious charges of educational incompetence were being made, than the purple prose of Welch or the dubious conclusions from Geddes' non-diagnostic test.

The teachers themselves were to gather and collate such data, together with additional information from secondary schools concerning the attainment of Tyndale children who had transferred. This information was to be accepted by the inquiry as 'agreed evidence', that is, the facts were agreed, but not the inferences. The ILEA's view was that no inferences could be drawn. Their position is understandable: the only inference that could emerge from the figures was that Tyndale was little different from any other ILEA school. Yet the ILEA's inspectors, without the benefit of the figures, because they had not sought them, had just implied in their reports that Tyndale was one of the worst schools in London. It was suggested in the inspection report that the school's expenditure showed a serious imbalance; but no figures were produced to support this contention. The staff, on the same evidence available to the inspectors, produced a schedule that showed no such imbalance. Its validity was never questioned by ILEA in the inquiry. But by that time not even the authority was relying heavily on its own inspection reports as evidence and, apart from Pape, called no member of the Junior inspection teams to give evidence. In the context of the inquiry, as it finally emerged, one wonders what the use of the inspection was.

On October 17th, when they met the managers' delegation, ILEA trod carefully, in order not to put themselves in an awkward legal position. Bramall had feared that litigation arising out of the Tyndale affair might go on for years. He may be proved right.

Chapter 14
The Press

An education authority's success is very much dependent upon its public image. Like all politicians, elected councillors who preside over an education authority depend upon a favourable image to ensure their re-election. Public interpretation of the realities of a particular situation assumes great importance. It is the press, radio and television that transmit to the public an interpretation of reality and it is thus that the 'media' is a paramount consideration for both a local authority and those wishing to influence its decisions.

In the Tyndale affair opposing parties were to realise the crucial nature of the press, and attempt to use it to their advantage. In particular, the managers used their media connections to manipulate crucial events. Yet the 'media' is not a neutral vehicle for others' opinions; it exercises an opinion and political rationale of its own. It has political axes to grind and wares to sell, and reality is interpreted to these ends.

During summer and autumn 1975 Fleet Street engaged in a political 'witch-hunt' against the Tyndale teachers of huge and vicious proportions. The campaign was such that the staff were forced several times to deny membership of any political party. However it was not to be solely directed against the Tyndale staff,

150

but all progressive educationalists and left-wing teachers.

In the case of Tyndale, the procedure was: blur the reality, then apply the conclusions to all schools, and to society. Relying on latent public prejudice against schools, the formula was to link incompetence with left-wing teachers with 'progressive' education; 'progressive' education was thus discredited as subversive and ineffectual. The national press, from the *Daily Express* to the *Guardian*, all employed this technique with varying degrees of subtlety and insidiousness.

The 'left' press adopted Tyndale, and attempted to interpret the teachers' victimisation in terms of their own party creed. Whilst the teachers were grateful for support the limited publication of these papers had only a minimal effect on the attitudes of parents or the ILEA. The weekly educational press refrained from taking sides, and through a meticulous coverage of the inquiry were to present a factual account of the proceedings, with little judgement or comment. One of the minor mysteries of the Tyndale saga was the attitude of the local *Islington Gazette*, which after showing an interest in the affairs of June and July 1975 barely covered the ensuing events. With a dispute of national interest on his doorstep one cannot imagine the editor disregarding its potential.

The press became involved in Tyndale surprisingly early. At the managers' meeting of October 1974 Conservative manager Norma Morris said she had been contacted by the *Evening Standard*, with a vague request for information about the school. This caused much agitation to the ILEA officers present. Rice indicated any such contacts were to be channelled to the ILEA press office.

In the relative calm of February 1975, Ellis was telephoned by Max Wilkinson of the *Daily Mail*. He said he had been informed at an education conference that Tyndale operated a policy whereby children could do as they wished ('total children's rights'?) and were able to select their teachers, those unpopular being moved out of the school. Ellis declined to comment, and the matter was dropped.

A chance meeting in June 1975 gave the teachers an opportunity of access to the press, but its failure to produce results underlines the press's reluctance to report issues from the 'wrong' political angle. A social meeting with a journalist from the *Guardian* resulted in the staff being promised an investigation into the rumouring and petitioning of this period, and the possibility of a large article if they so wished. Two weeks later the journalist informed the staff he could find no way into the story. In spite of having read the staff documents to date, he could not accept their assertions of political harassment. Perhaps he was to miss the scoop of the year. One month later his paper was able to publish the allegations of the managing body.

The most crucial press intervention, which was to dictate the future reporting of Tyndale, and which initiated the distortion of the school's educational reality, was prompted by the managers. Towards the end of June, Burnett fed the Hoodless critique of Tyndale to *The Times*. Having failed to influence Hinds directly, they were trying again by an indirect route. Whilst Burnett claimed the timing of the article was incidental, on the morning of the vital round table managers/teachers conference of July 2nd an article appeared entitled 'Teachers refuse to let managers into classrooms for inspection'.

After a resumé of the managers' case, there followed quotes from managers, and attacks on the school from 'background notes submitted to some sections of the press this week by managers'. Such deficiencies as 'a lack of reading schemes, music education and a lack of control of children outside the school' were cited. The political link was subtly introduced by a paragraph stating: 'The parents claim that that [the falling roll] is because the William Tyndale children are being taught by left-wing teachers who believe working class children should not be taught in the traditional methods.' The text makes it unclear whether this is a quote from Mabey, or the reporter's comment: There is no evidence of the parents had been contacted by *The Times*. The unfairness of the article must rest with the paper. No attempt was made to contact the Tyndale staff for comment before publication, and subsequent letters of protest and information were denied space by the letters editor.

The effect of this leak was devastating. The article and its background notes became the standard for all Tyndale articles. Criticisms cited were reiterated, until it appeared journalists were actually reporting each others' articles. These criticisms must have been firmly imprinted in the minds of the ILEA inspectorate when they made their reports on the school.

In the short term the Hinds meeting of that afternoon had been pre-empted. The deliberate escalation of the issue to a national level strictly on the managers' terms had meant that any peaceful reconciliation was impossible. It also had the effect of making the actual business of teaching at the school most difficult.

On July 2nd the school was besieged by reporters. Teachers were constantly having to answer the phone, or prevent the press from entering the building and harassing the children. The school gates were surrounded, and children had to run the gauntlet of questioning journalists. Teachers already under pressure from the stresses of inner-urban schooling, and a vicious campaign from their own managing body, were about to be submitted to a trial by a press which had already found them guilty. From that morning the press rarely left Tyndale: events occurred at such a rate they were never short of a headline.

That evening the parents were made aware of the 'subversion' that the press were claiming they asserted. Whilst *The Times* was used to influence ILEA, the *Evening News* carried the message to parents. 'Pop teachers ban managers in class' raved the headline. 'Pop music blared from a classroom at William Tyndale School' it alleged. The report gave selected instances of children making derogatory remarks about teachers, and attacked the alleged politics of the staff, claiming that 'the parents blame the falling roll on the fact that Tyndale teachers are too left wing'.

Thus the formula was born whereby progressives and left-wingers could be discredited under the same umbrella. The Tyndale pattern was set: a total disregard for the facts of the case; political smearing; and the interrogation of children for information about teachers.

The pressure continued to be applied by minor articles in the London evening press, reiterating Gittings' assertion that her son had played draughts all day at Tyndale.

On July 11th *The Times Educational Supplement* entered the fray. To its credit, it was the first paper to give an interview to the staff. Apart from a gratuitous section on McColgan's background, the article gave the managers' and teachers' points of view without comment. Tennant was quoted as saying he supported the school, but not some of the teachers. Hoodless spawned the notorious quotation that the teachers had created a 'ghetto school'. According to her, the only parents that remained were those who did not know how to get out.

This was to pale into a bedtime story compared with the
Evening News article of that afternoon. 'Is this a school or is it a

scandal?' demanded the headline of the full-page story by Linda Malvern, a freelance journalist. The meat of the article is made up of quotes from Hercules, and another of Gittings' friends, ex-parent Chasin. The school's policy is vilified, and Hercules makes the familiar political connection: 'It's political. There are a lot of militant people in that school. The headmaster has told me he is running a workers' school.' The reporter then generalises in the familiar way: 'People all over London have been concerned at the revolutionary teaching methods being introduced in the city's schools.'

Accompanying this 'insight' is a tabulated column entitled 'Could do better . . . The verdict on three pupils'. The *News* had sunk to soliciting parents to submit their children to 'independent' testing. An IQ test had been anonymously given to 4 pupils, and the results 'assessed' by a London psychiatrist. A vague and generalised analysis is recorded, to 'prove' that 75% of the children were underachieving, and would not pass the eleven plus examination (even if there had been one to pass). There is no information on the nature of the test used. No attempt is made at comparison or standardisation with other London schools. The social and emotional factors of the child's circumstances are ignored, and sweeping and damaging generalisations are made from a sample of four children.

The article also contained criticisms that became the clichés of later articles. The staff are likened to 'a load of hippies', and the sensational revelation is made that some teachers and children watched the Derby on television. Needless to say, in spite of Malvern spending over an hour on the phone asking the staff about their case, not one word of it was printed.

ILEA can never have had one of their schools thus maligned by the press. Yet no attempt was made by any official or member of the authority to defend the interests of the school or its employees. It is hardly surprising that the staff mistrusted the ILEA 'solution' announced to the press two weeks later.

The depth of damage this article did to parent/teacher relationships, particularly those of the prospective infant intake, can never be thoroughly fathomed. Just as Walker's campaign had reduced the roll the previous year, the press was to do likewise the next.

In order to protect the school against these alleged libels, Ellis 154 took up the matter with the NUT legal department. Subsequently libel proceedings were threatened against the *Evening News*, and the right to take similar action reserved against *The Times* for its article of July 2nd. During the summer vacation the *Daily Mail* was added to the list, for its allegations of political motivation in determining the children's education.

The ILEA's announcement of the intention to hold an inquiry preceded by an inspection punctuated press coverage during the summer recess, with occasional resumés of the managers' case. The inquiry would be into 'parent allegations of low educational standards'. No mention is made of it ever concerning itself with managerial conduct. The *Daily Express* even managed to resurrect Walker to comment adversely on the state of the school, which earned her a further solicitor's letter from the NUT.

In taking their decision to strike against the ILEA package, the teachers knew they would be subjecting themselves to crucifixion by the 'media'. They had tasted its venom the previous term, and were aware of its potential to alienate them from parental support. However this was an occasion when staff were initiating action, and whatever the consequences they had to put their case to the nation's press first.

A press statement was issued on September 21st to all national, local and educational papers, television stations, national and local radio. It clearly outlined the teacher's case: 'They were going on strike to press their demand for an independent inquiry into the management of the school, and into Labour Party involvement in attacks made on the staff and the school, and into the role of the ILEA in this whole affair'. There followed a list of demands, and an invitation to a press conference at a local Islington pub.

The response was almost total. For nearly two hours the staff re-iterated their case, and exhausted journalists' questions upon it. The next day scarcely one word of it was printed. Instead the education of the school and the politics of its staff were harangued in leader articles and editorials. Much attention was to be focused on the picket, and the political affiliations of those supporting it. Heartrending stories and photographs appeared, praising the dedication of Chowles and the torment of Walker at what was now dubbed 'The School of Shame'.

Contrived hysteria was to flow from Fleet Street all through the week, in trivial, incorrect and absurd articles abusing the teachers.

Perhaps the *Express* papers behaved worst of all. The *Daily Express* alleged one seven year old boy had run away from the inspectors at the school, crying 'I'm no blackleg.' According to the *Express*, the staff had taught the boy 'this kind of trade union language', whilst failing to teach him to read. That he had only been in the school three weeks was not explored. This article, typical of many, began: 'The allegations flew thick and fast outside the trouble-hit William Tyndale Junior School in London's Islington yesterday . . . of teachers smelling of drink after lunchtime pub sessions; of a child being hit on the head with a pair of scissors; of nine year olds still unable to read or write; of left-wing subversion by the teaching staff.' The following Sunday the *Express* attacked Ellis in scandalous fashion. He was described as 'a long haired git' who would be incapable of running a fish and chip shop'. His school, they maintained, taught the '3 R's of rebelliousness, rudeness and revolution'. Though the staff were already receiving poison pen letters, they did not expect them to be sanctioned by editors of national newspapers. Attempts at more serious articles such as the Sunday Times double page spread, were blighted by a bias towards the managers' position, no doubt due to their contacts and influence.

The immediate effect of the press reaction was to alienate perhaps one third of the parents, many of whom had signed the support petition two months earlier.

The following week the opening of Gaskin Street Strike School kept press interest alive, and if anything confused the situation, as it became more difficult to portray the staff as callous towards children. However, the main articles managed to revamp the previous weeks' distortions.

If the Tyndale teachers had been crucified during the strike, the managers' leak of the first inspection report was a public disembowelling. The managers had delivered the report to Fleet Street with military precision, even hiring taxis to do so. The purpose was to create such a public outcry that the strikers would not return to school. To that end they failed; but the report had given the press the 'evidence' it needed to put the final nail in the Tyndale coffin, and along with it 'progressive' education.

On October 16th 'The school of shame' once again hit the headlines. Inspector Welch's amazing revelations became editors' favourite catchwords: 'pupils aged nine and ten in William Tyndale Junior School are unable to spell simple words, use a ruler or write more than a few sentences'. More frightening for the staff were the hysterical quotes from parents, that the strikers would be lynched if they returned to school.

More sinister on this hysterical day was the behaviour of certain members of the press. Not only were children pressed into giving interviews about their teachers, but bewildered parents were gathered into groups by journalists, to pose in contrived angry stances for their photographs. One reporter shouted from the telephone box: 'Get me more interviews with anti-parents; my editor wants more anti-parents.'

The campaign now had the impetus it needed to attack left-wing teachers generally. A *Daily Express* editorial on October 18th read 'the exposure of the teaching methods and appalling results at William Tyndale School, London, has alerted parents everywhere to the need to find out what is going on in the classroom. This awareness is reinforced by the disclosure of sly political moulding of children's minds at another London school.'

Boyson, writing in the *Daily Telegraph*, demonstrated how Tyndale could be used to further a political Black Paper campaign. He opens his article 'How Red *are* our schools?' with a general attack on Rank and File, with its alleged International Socialist overtones, the cells he claims it has planted in London schools, and their supposed manipulation of union meetings in schools in the manner of 'the university student extremists'. He goes on to Tyndale, 'where Rank and File members and supporters took over a school to run it as a commune'. He continues: 'It is a favourite trick of the extreme left to destroy all values and all morality and to create what Trotsky called "Human dust" for the manipulation of the revolution.' The article concludes that 'the fall of 55% in the numbers of pupils at William Tyndale school shows that parents have little sympathy with the destructive pied pipers of our time. The introduction of the voucher system could destroy the left-wing extremists overnight, for the ordinary parent desires sound education and good moral values for his children.'

It did not come as a surprise the following Sunday when yet another Conservative MP, Angus Maude, predictably described the Tyndale staff as 'an arrogant bunch of International Socialists'. This article appeared beneath a cartoon depicting a bearded teacher being fed today's children through one eye, only for them to come out through the other as tomorrow's muggers!

Perhaps the Labour Party managers would have thought twice if they had known through which gutters their leaks were to run. Most of the press were now fighting all left-wing teachers and their supposed activities by encouraging parents to believe their children were suffering through modern teaching methods. But the Tyndale incompetence bandwagon had not ceased to roll: the untruths of the Hoodless documents were replaced by the subjective bias of the ILEA inspectorate.

Further press interest was stimulated by the inquiry. On its first morning Jill Tweedie in the *Guardian* set the trend, with an attack on progressive education à la Tyndale. She was to assert, with quotes from ancillary worker Horsman, who a year before had assisted Walker in her Black Paper campaign, that progressive education only catered for the middle classes. The attack had turned full circle.

Throughout the inquiry the press selected adverse evidence for their reports, and generally ignored the supportive, any samples of child misbehaviour being recorded with relish. A picture of All Hell at St Trinian's was painted from Hart's evidence, which reached its journalistic pinnacle with reports of Junior children 'exterminating' an Infant Dalek. When Walker testified, the reports seemed more like reviews of 'One flew over the cuckoo's nest', beneath her assertion that the school was like one vast, psychiatric clinic.

As the months passed the press gallery emptied. A brief revival came when the teachers gave evidence, but when it became apparent they were giving a spirited and intelligent account of themselves, the press withdrew. Only the educational press remained throughout, giving a balanced and factual account of events.

Perhaps on other issues some sections of the popular press can claim to be fair and enlightened. The witch-hunting of the Tyndale teachers will remain as an indictment against the so-called free press in Britain.

Chapter 15
The Inquiry

It was difficult for anyone in room 143 in County Hall on Monday, October 27th 1975 to believe they were witnessing an inquiry into the problems of one small primary school. The vastness and grandeur of the setting gave an impression of an event of greater proportions. The room, with an excellent view of the Thames, was spacious. At the front was a raised platform from which Chairman Auld presided; at the rear a public gallery, which though full at the beginning, soon emptied as the press and observers lost interest. Microphones were dotted about, relaying events to a press room elsewhere in the building.

To the right of Auld sat Dora Loftus, member of the Schools Sub-Committee and Chairwoman of managers of a South London school; to his left George Carter, head of Isaac Newton School, and teacher representative to the Sub-Committee. In front of Auld were the secretariat. Positioned directly beneath these three was the 'witness seat', from which all parties were to deliver their evidence.

Facing the platform, seated at long tables angled about the room, were the parties to the inquiry and their legal representatives. On one side the authority, represented by Edward Davidson. Behind them the managers, with their barrister Tessa Moorhouse. On the other side of the room sat the seven 'striking' teachers, represented by Stephen Sedley and his junior Richard Harvey; and the Infant staff and Chowles, both having the same barrister, Robert Spencer-Bernard, briefed by the NUT. These groups were added to as more parties became involved. The room was a confusion of documents.

Auld opened with an announcement that the panel of inquiry, originally five, had been reduced to three. The managers had objected to Leila Campbell, Labour member of the Sub-Committee, on the grounds that she had already shown herself to be prejudiced in the case. Reginald Watts, Conservative member of the Sub-Committee, could not attend for business reasons. There would have to be an adjournment to resolve the problem. Two hours later the inquiry was convened. Auld alone would be responsible for the proceedings and the report: Carter and Loftus merely advisers.

The confusion of documentation had become apparent. The teachers had been the only party to disclose all the evidence in their possession; whilst some parties had disclosed some documents, others had disclosed none. Some written statements of evidence had been received, others were not yet available. There was advantage to be gained from late submission of evidence, as statements could be tempered in response to assertions contained in earlier evidence. Auld ordered a complete 'discovery' of all files. He did not anticipate the problems this would produce.

At this point Walker made her presence felt. She had already submitted as her statement her letter of September 1974 to Rice. She now wished to become a party to the inquiry, suggesting she could represent herself, but Auld advised her to engage legal representation.

The proceedings finally got under way, with Davidson's opening speech. This consisted of a blow-by-blow account of the Education Officer's version of the events of the previous twenty months. Numerous other versions were to follow. Davidson portrayed the authority as the honest broker, trying to assist Auld with the relevant details. Even so, details of meetings and intrigues previously concealed were beginning to be uncovered. With this public confirmation of what had only been hinted at through rumour, the staff became more confident their case would be heard.

While everybody waited in anticipation for Davidson to finish, and the first witness to be called, another problem was in the making. Documents for duplication and distribution were pouring in   160 to the secretariat at such a rate that they could no longer cope. The lawyers were unable to prepare their cases adequately with new information arriving hourly. At the end of Davidson's speech, Auld called a private meeting with Counsel, and another adjournment, lasting one and a half weeks, was decided upon.

The Inquiry was reconvened on November 10th, only to meet with further difficulties. It had been set up on July 24th, and yet its terms of reference were still not defined, even though managers and staff had constantly asked for such clarification before the start. None of the parties seemed clear about the period to be considered — or indeed *what* was to be considered. Was the strike, which was concerned with this very matter, to be included? If it was to be omitted, what would happen to the first inspection report? If it was to be included the staff would be in triple jeopardy, as they might be faced with a disciplinary tribunal following the managers' complaint concerning the strike, and Briault's threat of prosecution for their actions during the first inspection. These questions were left in abeyance while Counsel took further instructions: They were resolved by an agreement to drop the managers' complaint and the threat of legal action, so that the strike period could be included. Auld declared the inquiry would be of a fact-finding nature, with no powers to make recommendations — disciplinary or otherwise.

In its eagerness to dispose of the affair the authority had anticipated an inquiry lasting no more than a week; it was now in its third week and the first witness of 100 had not been called. Auld tried to hasten the proceedings by cutting the afternoon tea break, but with the number of parties having increased — the London Borough of Islington was now represented by Jonathan Caplan, and Walker by John Williams — this measure seemed unlikely to improve matters.

The first witness for the authority was Rice, a quiet man who seemed nervous from the outset. Loftus peered down at him over the top of her glasses, and parties watched anxiously, trying to glean some indication of what the experience would be like. His cross-examination proceeded, with his agreeing with most of the criticisms of the school put to him by Moorhouse, and then, with equal emphasis, agreeing with the refutations of these put to him by Sedley. Unused to this type of close questioning on his work, he was no match for the skilled barristers. His ordeal did little to dispel the fears of future witnesses, and much to unnerve some. After six days as a witness he was released, looking older and exhausted, only to be recalled later at the request of Williams.

The pattern of questioning had been established, and the line of each party was becoming clear. Davidson, acting as if in charge, presented the position of the authority as one of helpful neutrality, trying to sort out the mess the managers and staff had got into, and taking no responsibility for it. He constantly reaffirmed the ILEA's concern for the children, its dependence on the responsibility of other adults in the running of its schools, and its impartiality.

The managers attacked Sedley's clients, while supporting Chowles and Austin (who was not represented at the inquiry). Their criterion for a good teacher seemed to be one who did not go on strike on September 22nd. They seemed to forget that the state of a school depends on all those who work in it, especially the deputy head. Their attack on Ellis was combined with a powerful attack on the authority for their inaction.

The seven teachers were forced into the position of defendants, being assailed from all sides. They maintained they were improving a difficult situation. Their efforts had been constantly frustrated by the interference of outside bodies. Even so the school had settled, and made progress.

Chowles and Hart, realizing their interests were not identical, were represented by different barristers — David Ellis representing Hart. They took up the roles of 'prosecutors' of Sedley's clients, while claiming they personally had nothing to answer for.

The other main party was Walker. In her violent attack on the methods of the seven teachers, and particularly on those of Ellis and Haddow, she took on the role of chief 'prosecutor', trying to expose the alleged revolutionary politics of the teachers, and their attempts at subversion.

The proceedings continued with all the solemnity and protocol of a courtroom. Any attempt at a joke was immediately quashed by Auld Cunningham described the inquiry in Parliament as being 'almost like a fashionable murder trial'. A letter had been received from Hedley Wales, refusing a request from ILEA to give evidence. Another letter was sent, emphasizing the importance of his attendance, as the person most closely connected with events both during Ellis' time and Head's. Davidson pointed out Wales could not be compelled to attend under the powers of the inquiry; as he no longer worked for the authority he was a 'free man'.

The inquiry was in its fourth week, and the second witness about to be called. Pape was treated as the 'great white god' of education, as his opinions were sought. He delivered his evidence with an authority and calmness that gave little away. Even so, he could not conceal his confusion over the administering of the Neale reading test, nor his anger at the disruption Sedley's clients had caused to the inspection — his last before retirement. He also failed to disclose his file, and caused Davidson embarrassment as new documents appeared, including a recently dated letter allegedly sent to Rice some months earlier.

Hinds was one of the Authority's final witnesses, answering questions with an admirably gentle evasiveness. He admitted to meetings with 'four angry ladies' from the managing body with such innocence, that anyone inexperienced in the ways of ILEA could not but wonder at his good-natured naivety. But the confident repartee with Counsel vanished at Sedley's suggestion that he had been colluding with the managers. 'I resent that' he retorted angrily, losing his earlier composure, which he was not to regain throughout his evidence. His annoyance reached its peak when a parent, a supporter of Ellis, stated that she too had some questions for him to answer.

The authority concluded its case with Buxton's evidence. His brash manner provided a contrast to Hinds. He opened his cross-examination with a declaration that he was not represented. He stated that Davidson had been engaged to represent the elected members of the authority, whose interests did not necessarily coincide with those of the paid officials. He required clarification of his position before he would answer questions. He adopted the same forcefulness throughout, as he discussed the workings of his 'patch'. He also admitted he might have said something to the effect that Ellis should be replaced by a 'right-wing, formal bastard', but that 'everyone has their little jokes'.

With the end of the authority's case the inquiry had reached its seventh week. No further response had been received from Wales or Head, who had also been invited to attend. New documents were arriving daily, and Auld's impatience increased. The view of the Thames was also obscured as Loftus began to feel the winter cold, and fastened the heavy blue curtains to prevent draughts.

Arrangements were being made for parents to attend. The managers, in their attempt to get as many critical parents as possible to give evidence, argued that copies of the documents should be deposited in Islington, and that evening sessions should be held there for parents who could not get to County Hall. Moorhouse insisted that all possible assistance should be given to this apparently helpless group of people, who it seems were terrified of the wrath of Ellis.

Cunningham, who to date had not attended the inquiry, shared this concern. He stated on November 5th in Parliament: 'There has been a claim for legal representations for the parents which, so far, has been rejected by the authority. In that formal setting the parents will have a problem in putting over their point of view. The inquiry is being held at County Hall, not in the area of the school, which means that parents will have difficulty in attending. Even if they go to County Hall it is possible that they will not get in, because the fifty or so seats are taken up by the press and TV.' The evening sessions were at best chaotic, and at worst a total waste of time, as many parents failed to turn up.

With the advent of the managers' case, whether through remembering other work to be done or as he was later to say 'time and money are of the essence', Auld's impatience increased even more. It was decided that to save time witnesses would no longer read their statements at the beginning of their evidence. Statements, which were still being submitted, were provoking other statements, and new evidence was being unearthed. Auld almost halted this flow by refusing the inclusion of any new evidence or statement without his approval. He complained of time-consuming lines of questioning, and objected to the inclusion of what he considered irrelevant evidence. Much of this involved cross-examination of those attacking the school, to determine their political motives.

Moorhouse's opening speech reaffirmed that the managers had only acted in the interests of 'those poor children'. The school had gone downhill, and the authority had refused to act. The force of her attack was directed at the authority. Burnett was the first witness: she looked pale and ill, and extremely nervous. She said parents had come to her with complaints, but she could only think of four names, two of which also belonged to managers. She had been ill, and had not been involved in the meetings with Hinds, but had circulated the petition when she had become angry with the staff, even though she could see it was harmful to the school. She had difficulty in explaining her contact with Walker.

Burnett was followed by Dewhurst and Gittings, both giving

164

passionate accounts of the state of the school, both having been involved in many secret meetings, and both having had contact with Walker in June 1974. Gittings revealed her friendship with Hercules, and that she may have suggested to at least one parent that letters of complaint be written to Divisional Office. She was the first of the managers to reveal the organization of the leak of the first inspection report to the press, in which she was a prime mover. These activities had previously been concealed from the staff.

Difficulties arose in the managers' case when Martindale appeared as a witness. He clearly had no knowledge of the secret managerial goings on, even though he was a manager of long standing and had attended most official meetings. He seemed disturbed at some events, and Moorhouse found herself wishing to cross-examine her own witness.

The managers fell into three broad categories: those active in the dispute, such as Gittings, Dewhurst and Burnett; those who joined the attack at a later date, such as Mabey, Tennant, Fairweather and Hoodless; and those who knew next to nothing of the affair until the events of summer 1975, such as Morris, Bolland and Roberts.

Mabey had done his homework on the subject of management, and his main attack was directed at the authority. He pointed to the lack of managerial power, especially in a situation of conflict; it seemed obvious that many of his actions in relation to Tyndale were designed to expose these inadequacies by setting up confrontation. He expressed a desire to change the system, which works only as long as no problems arise.

Tennant portrayed his position as that of the middle man, entering the conflict at its height and trying to straighten things out. He agreed with the line that the school was a mess, but had managed to keep out of the intrigues. He acted as if he couldn't see what all the fuss was about, and almost laughed at the suggestion anyone could be trying to get rid of Ellis. He showed dexterity in fending off awkward questions, though there were some confusion and arguments, over the notes of a meeting with Hinds, as to whether Tennant had described the teachers as being 'anarchic' or 'anarchistic', and whether it was to be spelt with a large or small 'a'.

Fairweather denied having given the staff the version of the July 23rd meeting at Divisional Office that they claimed she had. She also denied having 'early' knowledge of the petition, although this was later refuted by Page, who remembered discussing the matter in her presence in the members' bar at County Hall after the meeting with Hinds. She could not remember any meeting with Hoodless where they had discussed visiting Hinds as Labour Party representatives, although Miles, former parent manager, remembered this conversation. She was quite sure, contrary to Ellis' evidence, that she had not visited the school on the morning of the May 19th managers' meeting.

Hoodless was the final managers' witness. Her quiet voice and demure manner belied the intrigues she had apparently been involved in. Since her appointment she had taken a major part in every attack on the school, though she had never officially visited it. At the suggestion that Hoodless had been 'planted' on the Tyndale managing body, Loftus angrily intervened, stating that Hoodless was appointed legitimately. Hoodless experienced her most embarrassing moments during other people's evidence. Bolland, who had stated his opposition to the petition, was to change his evidence after a break in which Hoodless talked to him. Unfortunately she had been overheard. She was also taken outside for a reminder not to interfere with other witnesses' evidence during Chowles' cross-examination.

Attempts Auld made to speed up the proceedings, by the substitution of a written list of those involved in the distribution of the petition, wasted more time. There were arguments as to which questions were still admissible, the list itself, provided by the managers, never having been completed. It had also been revealed that the original of the petition, diligently sought after by the teachers, had been 'lost' by the authority, and all efforts to find it had failed. The staff were never to discover to whom the illegible signatures belonged, or to whom the petition should have been returned, or whether all the original sheets had been photo-copied.

During the last days of the managers' case a letter of resignation was received by Ellis, from Richards. The affair had been too much, and she felt she could no longer be involved in it. Around this time a Christmas tree could be seen rising up over Davidson's shoulder, as it was placed on the Embankment.

Still the Inquiry showed no indication of nearing a close. Parents' evidence was being heard in the evenings. However parents failed to turn up on so many occasions that some sessions had to be curtailed, while others consisted of a series of brief adjournments. Many parents made accusations against the teachers to the press and

166

in statements to the inquiry, yet were unwilling to attend to back up accusations with evidence. None of the parents who had sent complaints to the authority gave evidence to the inquiry, and neither did Hercules.

Every effort was made to cater for parents. Barristers were asked to remain seated while questioning them, for fear of intimidation — and Ellis was asked to move further away from a witness. Parents who did not turn up were written to, suggesting a new time for their attendance. Still they did not arrive. This extension of the working day severely hit the lawyers, who were coping with hurried briefings and the transportation of documents. The sessions were not adequately utilized, and after three weeks were discontinued.

Some parents who had viciously attacked the school seemed to know little about it. The same theme occurred with monotonous regularity in their statements. Parents liked the Infant school, did not like the Junior, and would remove their children if Ellis returned. During cross-examination some agreed they had been satisfied prior to the strike, and some had even signed a petition in support of the staff in July 1975. Parents who had been friendly with staff and had helped in the school had become hostile, but seemed at a loss to explain their change of heart.

Amongst this group so willing to condemn Ellis were some whose children had only been in the school for three weeks, having transferred from the Infants' in September 1975. It seemed their children had been transformed in this short time by the methods in the Juniors'. Their work and behaviour had apparently deteriorated beyond all recognition.

Sedley's clients had no opportunity to answer many allegations against them, as they had not been in statements previously submitted, and were often introduced after the relevant teachers had completed their evidence. As more parents presented evidence, it became obvious that many were basing judgements on the same old stories about the school, rather than on personal knowledge.

Many parents gave evidence in support of the staff, and praised their work highly. Some would not allow their children back if Ellis did *not* return.

As their evidence was heard, the different treatment of different groups of parents became noticeable. The anti-parents had been cosseted and protected on all fronts; supportive parents were not treated so gently. One was accused of being a liar by Walker's counsel; another was asked by Spencer-Bernard if he was married to his wife. It seemed these parents were considered 'guilty by association'.

Ellis was called on the last afternoon before the Christmas recess. He was to remain in the witness chair for a total of ten days, the longest of any witness. At this point the questioning changed from the intrigues at County Hall and the Islington Labour rooms to a detailed discussion of educational aims and practice, combined with a political interrogation. How many teachers would cope with explaining their methods and educational philosophies in such detail? The lawyers, including Auld, had little understanding of teaching methods, and much time was wasted explaining the simplest things in minute detail. Sinister motives were attributed to the simplest of changes. Many of the legal representatives had no concept of what a London school was really like; Ellis was constantly having to justify misdemeanours of a type that happens regularly in such schools. The lawyers did not appear to know other schools faced behavioural problems and had non-readers, and simply asked why Tyndale did.

The political line of questioning was more sinister. This came principally from Chowles and Walker. Ellis was not only questioned on his own beliefs and affiliations, but also on Haddow's. Refusal to answer such questions was greeted by Auld with an instruction to do so in the interests of the inquiry. Auld seemed able to see a relevance to political questioning that he had not seen earlier. Accusations of indoctrination had to be defended, views on society justified.

The second witness for the staff was McWhirter, who was to be questioned for over two days. One of the few teachers who had worked under Head and Ellis, she was questioned about the comparable states of the school; but more time was spent with questions about Haddow's beliefs and practices within the school. Being the NUT representative she was also interrogated by Davidson, about the strike period, although he had not introduced this subject into Ellis's cross-examination by Moorhouse It was during McWhirter's cross-examination that Loftus could contain her annoyance no longer. After a sudden outburst, saying it was her private time being wasted, the inquiry was adjourned for a few minutes.

Following McWhirter came Haddow, also to be questioned for over two days. His cross-examination involved not only an attack on his alleged political motivation, but also a retrial of William Blake, in

168

order to prove he was a revolutionary, and thus prove Haddow was also, through his use of the 'tyger' quotation. Discussions followed as to which critique of Blake could be taken as the 'orthodox version'.

With Felton the lawyers explored the 'ringleader' theory, trying to prove he knew little of the affair, but was being led by Haddow and Ellis.

McColgan was to face another line of attack. Her membership of Rank and File interested some parties considerably, in particular ILEA. She was taken through the aims of the organization one by one, and asked if she agreed with them. Parties seemed quite disappointed when they discovered she was not trying to wreck schools.

The final witness of the six teachers was Green. She had also been at the school with Head and was questioned, particularly by the Infants' counsel, about the alleged deterioration of the school, which she emphatically refuted.

The parties for the prosecution had not succeeded in isolating Ellis and Haddow from the rest of the teachers; a picture had been built up of a group of well-informed teachers concerned in the running of the school.

At this point the room was blacked out, the chairs rearranged, and parties settled down for the showing of the film about the school which had been made by students from Paddington. Paul Connett, leader of the project, was later to say in evidence that he was impressed by the organization of the school.

After the teachers' case came that of Chowles. She was deputy head in a school which she claimed was in a mess. It had been her task to co-ordinate the system of Tuesday options, operated in 1974 and 1975, although she asserted that these did not work. She claimed that nobody had told her what to do. She obviously did not agree with her colleagues' views on education, and supported Walker's, while calling herself a progressive.

She said Ellis had brought 'class consciousness' to Tyndale, that she felt it was all right for children to question things, but objected when they wanted to do something about it.

After Chowles came Hart, the only member of staff to appear for the infant school in an inquiry which was, ostensibly, into the workings of both schools. She was confident she had nothing to defend, with her exceptional inspection report, and the glowing praise she had received from other witnesses. It was in her obsessiveness in sticking exhibits on card, and the cataloguing of the misdemeanours of Junior children, which she reported to Divisional Office without Ellis' knowledge, that she was challenged. A stream of accusations against the teachers came forth, which, not having been put to them by her barristers in their cross-examinations, they had no means of answering. She had difficulty in explaining her connections with Ford, and denied the meetings which Ford remembered, and the political allegations she had made to her about the Junior staff.

At this point a letter was received from Head saying he 'wanted nothing to do with the patently grubby affair'. Other witnesses to appear included Hurwitz, the local librarian, who excitably described her knowledge of Tyndale. The St Trinian's picture she painted of Haddow's class which, she claimed, was so noisy at the library that the deaf caretaker complained, was so amusing that parties had to be warned to behave properly.

Lendon, one-time supporter of the staff (represented by Spencer-Bernard), said he had not advised Ellis to lock out the managers, and had advised him as a head, not a Union official.

Howell, councillor and Infant parent, gave evidence as an expert witness for the managers. Extracts from his book on school management were introduced as formal evidence, and he proceeded to 'prove' that all that the managers had done, including the petition, was completely reasonable. He used his book to illustrate this, even though the similarities between the situation cited and the activities of the managing body were less than obvious.

Amongst other witnesses was Newman, former parent manager, who appeared for Ellis to register his disgust at the actions of the managing body. It was in response to Newman's evidence that Chowles was to submit a statement saying she had hit a child.

Austin also gave evidence for the teachers. He described the team teaching at Tyndale, and felt it had run more smoothly than a scheme he had been involved in at another school, which Pape had praised in an ILEA 'occasional paper' on education.

Finally, Walker appeared. Subdued at first, she got more excitable as she became confused by Sedley. Her evidence was riddled with irrelevancies, such as the friends she had who had seen psychiatrists, and the scrap metal merchant she had known in Kensington. At the beginning of her evidence the press reappeared, hoping to get another good story about the teachers. Political accusations followed, but however much Walker insisted on her lack of political motivation and neutrality, she could not hide her own political position.

On the last day of her evidence, as the proceedings were winding down, she suddenly announced that yet another bag of documents was in existence, lying somewhere in her greenhouse. When Williams apologised, saying this was unfortunate, Auld could control his anger at the length of proceedings no longer. 'It's not unfortunate,' he thundered, 'It's disgraceful.' These papers were rushed to the inquiry, and parties spent another late evening at County Hall, waiting for the documents to be photocopied. The teachers at least were not disappointed. Not only did they contain details of Walker's campaign, including names, addresses and telephone numbers of parents, but also correspondence with Boyson concerning the alleged subversion of the school. (A letter was subsequently sent to the House of Commons inviting Boyson to attend — an invitation he was to refuse.) There were also numerous drafts of documents.

The final speeches were now heard. Perhaps the most significant of these was Davidson's. He blamed the managers for their interference and Ellis for the running of the school. He felt there was nothing which could have been done by the authority earlier in the dispute, and disclaimed all responsibility on their behalf. Even Auld became confused by his assertions, and ended up cross-examining him about his final speech.

At the beginning of Davidson's speech, Cunningham made his first appearance at the inquiry — as an observer. He was the only observer who made a point of introducing himself to Auld. He sat while Davidson's summing-up attacked the school but, the moment ILEA turned its guns on the managers, he rose and walked rapidly from the inquiry, slamming the door behind him.

When Davidson sat down, the proceedings were at an end. Auld thanked everybody for coming, although some felt they had had no choice. The teachers departed onto paid leave, to await Auld's findings, which ILEA said would be available in April. Whatever those findings may be, they will not be the last chapter in the Tyndale story.